CultureShock!

A Survival Guide to Customs and Etiquette

Italy

Raymond Flower
Alessandro Falassi

Marshall Cavendish
Editions

This edition published in 2008 by:
Marshall Cavendish Corporation
99 White Plains Road
Tarrytown, NY 10591-9001
www.marshallcavendish.us

Other Marshall Cavendish Offices:
Marshall Cavendish International (Asia) Private Limited. 1 New Industrial Road, Singapore 536196 ■ Marshall Cavendish Ltd. 5th Floor, 32–38 Saffron Hill, London EC1N 8FH, UK ■ Marshall Cavendish International (Thailand) Co Ltd. 253 Asoke, 12th Flr, Sukhumvit 21 Road, Klongtoey Nua, Wattana, Bangkok 10110, Thailand ■ Marshall Cavendish (Malaysia) Sdn Bhd, Times Subang, Lot 46, Subang Hi-Tech Industrial Park, Batu Tiga, 40000 Shah Alam, Selangor Darul Ehsan, Malaysia

Marshall Cavendish is a trademark of Times Publishing Limited

ISBN 10: 0-7614-5486-1
ISBN 13: 978-0-7614-5486-1

Please contact the publisher for the Library of Congress catalog number

Printed in China by Everbest Printing Co Ltd

Photo Credits:
All black and white photos from Raymond Flower except for pages 7, 8, 42, 64–65, 88–89, 103, 129, 140–141, 161, 172–173, 184–185, 198–199, 224–225, 241 (Lonely Planet Images); pages viii–ix, xiii, 36–37, 60–61, 147, 153, 170, 190–191, 245, 264–265 (Corel Stock Photo Library); pages 12–13, 24–25, 74, 86, 110–111, 137 (Pietro Scòzzari).
Colour photos from Getty Images pages b–c, f–g, p; Photolibrary pages a, d–e, h, i, j–k, l, m, n–o ■ Cover photo: Photolibrary

All illustrations by TRIGG

ABOUT THE SERIES

Culture shock is a state of disorientation that can come over anyone who has been thrust into unknown surroundings, away from one's comfort zone. *CultureShock!* is a series of trusted and reputed guides which has, for decades, been helping expatriates and long-term visitors to cushion the impact of culture shock whenever they move to a new country.

Written by people who have lived in the country and experienced culture shock themselves, the authors share all the information necessary for anyone to cope with these feelings of disorientation more effectively. The guides are written in a style that is easy to read and covers a range of topics that will arm readers with enough advice, hints and tips to make their lives as normal as possible again.

Each book is structured in the same manner. It begins with the first impressions that visitors will have of that city or country. To understand a culture, one must first understand the people—where they came from, who they are, the values and traditions they live by, as well as their customs and etiquette. This is covered in the first half of the book.

Then on with the practical aspects—how to settle in with the greatest of ease. Authors walk readers through how to find accommodation, get the utilities and telecommunications up and running, enrol the children in school and keep in the pink of health. But that's not all. Once the essentials are out of the way, venture out and try the food, enjoy more of the culture and travel to other areas. Then be immersed in the language of the country before discovering more about the business side of things.

To round off, snippets of basic information are offered before readers are 'tested' on customs and etiquette of the country. Useful words and phrases, a comprehensive resource guide and list of books for further research are also included for easy reference.

CONTENTS

Chapter 7
Enjoying the Culture 149

Chapter 8
Learning the Language 209

Chapter 9
Working in Italy 231

Chapter 10
Fast Facts about Italy 247

FOREWORD

'Simply letting yourself live is beautiful in Italy... what, after all, is pleasure if not an extraordinary sweet pain?'

—*Heinrich Heine*

As your plane circles over the Eternal City on its descent into Leonardo da Vinci Airport, you may perhaps catch a glimpse of such famous landmarks as the Tiber, St Peter's or the Colosseum in the urban sprawl below.

"*Tutte le strade portano a Roma* (All roads to Rome)", smiles your neighbour as you fasten your seat belts and check your belongings in preparation for the landing.

It's an exciting moment. Yet naggingly, a small voice deep inside you keeps murmuring: "What's in store for me down there... what will Italy really be like?" You think of all the old chestnuts you've heard about Italy, and wonder how you'll cope with a strange new environment. In other words, you fear you're in for a cultural jolt. And of course you are right: things will certainly be different from what you are used to at home. What else do you expect?

But there's no need to worry. Italians are past masters in the art of making visitors feel over the moon. They have always been ready to welcome the invader—provided he comes with a smile on his face. The cultural differences you encounter will prove exhilarating if you remain as cheerful and upbeat as the Italians themselves.

So the first tip we have to offer is to greet Italy with a smile. That's the secret. A smile is enough!

ITALIAN FACTS AND FIGURES

Since these introductory remarks are addressed to the first-time visitor, we'd better start by stating a few basic facts. Italy is a mountainous land mass nearly 1,300 km (807.9 miles) long and roughly 250 km (155.3 miles) wide, stretching from the great arc of the Alps to half-way across the Mediterranean.

Its silhouette is unique—a high-heeled riding boot poised to kick Sicily through the straits between Tunisia and

Sardinia. No other country is so immediately recognisable on the map.

In contrast to the glaciers which form its frontier to the north, most of Italy is bordered by the sea, with a coastline extending over 1,600 km (994.2 miles) (the distance from London to Rome). Seventy per cent of the country is mountainous, which restricts the fertile areas and affects the climate. Yet 70 per cent of the land is cultivated, and always has been, which says a lot for the centuries-old ingenuity of the people.

This disparity, accentuated by Italy's length, explains the difference in temperament that distinguishes the inhabitants of the highly industrialised north from those in the Mediterranean Mezzogiorno.

CAMPANILISMO AND IDENTITY

Italy is one nation, to be sure. But at the same time it is also two countries—north and south—indeed three if you count the centre separately, or even five if the islands of Sicily and Sardinia are reckoned apart. In fact it is more like 20 countries if you consider the true spirit of each region.

This psyche was personified by the ancient Romans in a *genius loci*—a spirit that inhabited and guarded the different localities—and Italians still tend to identify themselves most closely with their native place or their vital spaces.

What they call *campanilismo* is the love for, and identification with, that geographic and human space which is visible from the bell-tower of their own town or village. With growing intensity they give their loyalty to the Country, the Region, the Town, the Family and (ultimately) the Self. Which means to say that a Sienese for instance, will feel himself or herself to be an Italian when abroad, a Tuscan when in Italy and a Sienese while in Tuscany.

But it's only when he is safely in sight of his city walls that the Sienese feels truly himself—and even then he will be most comfortable within the confines of his own *contrada* (ward), surrounded by the testimony of his personal and family background. However sociable they may be, Italians are above all individualists, just as Italy itself is manifestly

Venice is one of Italy's landmark cities and a great attraction for tourists.

a land of contrasts. This may sound like a cliche, (after all, every country is full of contrasts) but it is a fact that must be emphasised. The point is for us to discern which are the relevant contrasts, and how these inconsistencies can affect your daily life in Italy.

CONTRASTS

Italy is a very new nation with a very old civilisation. It is fragmented into a kaleidoscope of regional cultures, all strong and deeply rooted in a land approximately the size of California, and which until 1860 was a myriad of different states at war or at odds with each other. Consider some of these contrasts:

- Here is a country which is the seat of the Holy Church, yet which has fostered the development of the strongest left-wing sub-culture (first anarchist, then socialist and communist) that has been seen in western Europe during the past century.
- While showing a strong deference to tradition in every shape and form, it has nurtured such high-tech enterprises as Fiat, Olivetti, Augusta helicopters, Beretta firearms, and for 30 years has averaged the highest growth rate in Europe. (Today Italy ranks seventh among industrialised nations.)
- Parts of the south are still poverty-stricken, yet Lombardy is the third richest province in Europe.
- In the post-war years, its governments have lasted on average less than 12 months, yet with the same political leaders maintaining a sort of life-time tenure of power that only ended when the Clean Hands revolution and election in March 1994 brought new faces to the fore.
- The strong ties of the Italian family are proverbial and family values form the background of Italian society even in times of turmoil. Yet, according to recent statistics, the average Italian family comprises 2.6 members.
- Italy is reputed to have the most beautiful architecture in the world. Yet its coastline is marred by the most

striking examples of 'savage building', and many of its suburbs are indistinguishable from the purgatorial outskirts of Paris, New York, Moscow or Tokyo.

- In a single day by train or by car, you can travel from the high Alps to Sicily, thereby experiencing the full spectrum of European scenery—which itself is probably the most varied on earth.
- Italian people are known to be good-natured, easy-going, fun-loving extroverts. But while you are unlikely to notice it, violence is endemic beneath the surface.
- In the words of Italy's own ministry of interior, Sicily, Calabria and Campania are regions where 'law and order are at stake'.
- Italian cooking is acclaimed throughout the world. Yet fast food is spreading insidiously in Italian towns and is increasingly popular with the younger generation.

Either directly or indirectly, people relate daily to these contrasts and you will by necessity have to deal with them. They should be regarded not as obstacles, but as means to understanding—and therefore appreciating—this beguiling land.

We hope that you will come to feel, like the authors, that these disparities represent not only the character of Italy but also its essential appeal. Maybe they are even symbolic of the general human condition today.

AN INVERTED FUNNEL

This book is intended to be a companion, not a guide. It has been planned as an inverted funnel, or loud-speaker if you like, which progressively broadens and amplifies the themes.

After kicking off with a few points you need to know at the start, we'll move on to more general matters, such as learning the language, getting around the country, appreciating the different regional dishes, seeing how Italians live, understanding their attitudes and customs, tackling the problems of setting up a home, as well as those of working and doing business in Italy. In short, of interacting with Italians and their culture.

What's more, since the chief reason why many visitors come to Italy is to enjoy that culture, we shall include a special section designed to brief you quickly on Italian history, literature and, of course, the arts.

That's the menu. *Buon Appetito!*

Many old towns and villages dot the landscape.

MAP OF ITALY

FIRST IMPRESSIONS

CHAPTER 1

'Italia! Oh Italia! Thou who hast the fatal gift of beauty!'
—Lord Byron

Foreign travel is a challenge, an engagement of yourself against an entirely new environment. You want to find transport at the airport or a taxi at the station which will take you to your hotel. There you want to receive a friendly reception, a room ready with the right voltage, enough coat-hangers, a hot shower, cool sheets, sufficient towels, some glasses and a view.

You want to be provided with a proper cup of tea, strong coffee or strong drink, matches you can strike and local currency for your dollars, pounds or yen. You want to find the shops open and dinner being served whether it's still only 6.30 pm or well after 10:00 pm. You want to be entertained, but you also want to be left in peace.

You want to find everything just as you expected, only better. You're also looking for the unexpected, but it must be something you can cope with. You don't want to be caught unawares, or worse still, to look like a fool. You want to feel knowledgeable, competent and thoroughly at ease.

In fact, you're a bundle of needs at the mercy of clerks behind counters, porters, waiters, keys that don't seem to fit and money you don't understand. That's the practical side of culture shock, and we must see what we can do about it.

ARRIVAL

The first Italians you are likely to meet are the smartly turned out immigration and customs officers who will either greet you with a courteous smile, or wave you through with a nonchalant gesture. Nothing to worry about so long as your papers are in order and you're not carrying around a tobacconist's shop or any prohibited items such as drugs.

GETTING FROM THE AIRPORT TO TOWN

The taxi driver may try to rip you off, so it is as well to find out in advance what the standard fare is. The airline will let you know. Pay what's indicated on the meter and add a small tip. Do not pay any additional charge if it's not indicated. As most airports are not far from the city it won't be a long ride (Pisa International is barely a mile from the centre). But Leonardo da Vinci Airport, or Fiumicino as it's also called, is over 18 miles from the centre of Rome.

The buses that used to run from the airport to the main railway station have been replaced by smart yellow trains that come right into the airport, and will take you to the Termini in under half an hour, making a few stops on the way. Quicker than by taxi, to be sure. Just cross the enclosed bridge outside the arrival building, and buy your ticket at the entrance to the sleek airport station. You can also get tickets to other destinations there. (Don't forget to 'validate' your ticket by punching it in the stamping machine before boarding the train.)

Florence has at last upgraded its Peretola airfield into an international airport, used by an increasing number of European flights. Even so, Pisa remains Tuscany's main airport, and there again a swanky single-class train whisks you to Florence in precisely an hour, every hour.

Milan's alternate airport, Malpensa, which also serves Turin, has also been upgraded. But as it's far from both cities, you may prefer to take the bus or train rather than hire a taxi. Amenities are fast improving there, so enquire on arrival. Linate airport is within easy reach of the city centre.

ACCOMMODATION

There are plenty of hotels in Italy which are up to world-class standards and provide top-rate accommodation, service and facilities, for which they charge you through the nose.

There are also a large number of hotels in the first-class category which tend to justify their status by going in for over-plush decorations and an obsequious, often rather snooty, attitude towards guests to cover up the shortcomings of the service they offer. It is a well-known fact, as any hotelier will confirm, that European standards of service are no longer on a par with, say, Southeast Asia, because of the high cost of labour, social security, restrictive practices and so forth which plagues Italy more than most countries.

REASONABLE HOTELS

Unless you have to keep up appearances for business reasons or don't mind what you spend, you may find it preferable to stay in one of the numerous Category 2 establishments.

These are very much the same wherever you go. There are usually several in each city, all bleakly modern-looking from the outside and reminiscent of an AGIP motel, which seems to serve as a universal pattern.

The entrance hall doubles as reception area, TV lounge and coffee shop combined. There will probably be only one lift and maybe you'll be expected to lug your luggage up to your room which will be sparsely fitted out with shiny modern furniture. But it will be immaculately clean, the beds will be comfortable, the bathroom gleaming, the water piping hot, and there will even be an ashtray with someone's advertisement on it.

The atmosphere will be nothing to write home about, and it won't be particularly cosy. But hotels of this type are usually much more friendly than their grander counterparts. Often they are privately-owned establishments, run by the family with not much outside help. Because of this their costs are relatively low and they don't have to overcharge.

The management will take a personal interest in you and help you with your problems. They'll advise you where to go and how best to get there. They'll even give you tips about shopping in the vicinity.

In all probability, the hotel will have a restaurant attached which caters for the locals and therefore offers good food. You'll be glad to get back to the familiar surroundings and people you know after a long day of sightseeing. On the whole, you'll reckon it's a good bet, especially when the time comes to pay the bill.

BREAKFAST

If you are used to a hearty breakfast in the morning, then you are in for your first surprise.

Italians, like most Mediterranean people, don't go in for breakfast. They don't like starting the day on a full stomach and make do with a tiny cup of strong coffee along with a pasta, which in this case means a croissant or a pastry.

The most you're likely to get in the hotel, as a concession to the curious foreign habit of demanding breakfast, is a cappuccino with rusks and a little pot of jam, served at the bar in the entrance hall or in a small hidden room.

If you happen to prefer tea, you'll find that isn't an Italian speciality either. It will be made with a tea-bag in a coffee cup filled with water heated up in the coffee machine, and served with a slice of lemon. Ask for a pot of tea and you'll

get double that amount. Milk will be produced only on request. To be fair it should be added that some hotels, in a genuine attempt to cater for foreigners' needs (and perhaps scenting a useful source of revenue) have begun to lay on a notional buffet breakfast, from which you can help yourself to a glass of juice and a plate of cornflakes along with the rusks and jam.

But when in Rome, why not do as the Romans do? Which is to step outside and go to the nearest café for a cappuccino and a bun. At least you'll be soaking up a bit of local colour.

Stepping outside provokes another jolt. You will feel deafened by the sheer noise generated by the teeming sidewalks (too narrow to be called pavements!) and all those little Fiats aggressively revving their engines as they try to squeeze down the street.

It may take you a little time to edge your way through the traffic and reach the café. There, like any old hand, you will first pay for the *scontrino* (ticket) at the cash desk and then hand it to the man behind the counter as you give him your order.

In the same way as the smartly dressed women and prosperous looking businessmen (or are they lawyers, even politicians?) who are queuing up alongside, you will be expected to drink your coffee standing up. That is, unless you pay extra to sit at a table where you can cast an eye over the morning papers and indulge in the favourite Roman pastime of watching the people go by.

PEOPLE-WATCHING

The first thing that will strike you is how elegant Italians are, especially if you happen to be seated at a table on the pavement in the famous Via Veneto, which is the chic place to go.

There's no doubt that the Italians have style, not only in what they wear but also how they move. (We'll talk about body language later on.) If you spot people wearing loud clothes or discordant colours, they're probably from Hollywood or Las Vegas.

Italians enjoy relaxing in the *piazza*, as seen here in the Piazza del Duomo, Orvieto, Umbria.

PANINI

BRUSCHETTE

BIRRA E VINO

Bars, like this one at Piazza della Signoria, Florence, are popular amongst locals and tourists alike.

HAVING A MEAL

Like most Mediterranean people, Italians eat only twice a day. Steering clear of breakfast and anything at tea-time, they concentrate on lunch and dinner. For them, *pranzo* and *cena* are the high spots of the day.

An Italian Meal

The menu for both meals is virtually the same. Both tend to consist of *antipasto*, usually a selection of cold cuts, which as the name suggests, comes before a copious pasta or rice dish, known as *il primo*. *Il secondo* is the main course, either meat, fowl or fish, with vegetables and salad served separately. Then comes cheese, often a single variety, followed by *dolce* (sweet or dessert) and/or fruit. The meal is concluded with a tiny cup of espresso (not cappuccino).

On the whole Italians don't go in for cocktails, though sometimes they take an aperitif, usually some sort of vermouth or a glass of white sparkling wine. But normally they start off with wine and continue drinking it right through the meal, maybe finishing off with a so-called *digestivo*, that is to say an *amaro* or a *grappa* (both of which are liqueurs). Oddly enough—to Anglo-Saxon eyes—they may end up with a single whisky on the rocks.

People don't necessarily go the whole hog twice a day. But certainly in restaurants they tend to take an *antipasto,* a *primo*, a *secondo* accompanied by a single vegetable or salad and an espresso. Sometimes they skip the *antipasto* or the *dolce*. But they nearly always have pasta (or occasionally soup) before the main dish.

These items are all listed separately on the menu, which can be confusing to foreigners who are used to being offered a set meal with everything already included.

Menu Turistico

Many restaurants do indeed make available a set meal called

Wine

Most restaurants, certainly most *trattorias*, offer wine by the carafe, which is usually both good and cheap and can be diluted with water if you wish—many people do it. Ask for a *fiasco* of *vino del padrone, vino sfuso* or *vino della casa*. This goes down better in a *trattoria* than a restaurant though.

menu turistico, but it is usually not very inspiring. Swiss and German visitors who are accustomed to eating a single copious dish with all the trimmings are often dismayed to find that they have to wade through several courses and, having ordered a variety of vegetables with their main course, discover that these are served (and charged for) separately. They complain that it is an expensive business. (Conversely, when Italians go to Switzerland or Germany, they tend to order a series of dishes, each of which is designed to be a whole meal, and find this an expensive business too.)

Eating Light

If you want to have something light, the best thing to do is smile at the waiter, explain you're on a diet, and order just a pasta or a meat dish with a salad to go with it. The management may be disappointed, but after all they do make a cover charge.

Equally, if you can't face a bottle of wine in the middle of the day, order a bottle of mineral water or some beer (Italians are becoming quite keen on beer).

The difference between a *trattoria* and a restaurant is really a question of comfort, looks, cuisine and cost. If you want to splurge, go to a posh restaurant. If not, choose a *trattoria*. It will be simpler and more down to earth, offering *casalinga* (just the way mama makes it) cooking, but if other Italians are eating there the food is bound to be good. The establishment wouldn't last long if they weren't.

In most towns there is also the *Tavola Calda*, which are self-service places where you can choose whatever you like, and these are usually good value if a bit short on charm. Another good bet for a quick snack is simply the bar. Many bars offer ham rolls or *un tost*, which is a hot toasted ham and cheese sandwich. The smarter Motta and Allemagna bars have some juicy sandwiches called *tramezzini*. And—one hates to mention it—there are now the fast food chains, though you surely haven't come to Italy for a Big Mac? There is in fact an Italian alternative to the hamburger chains. The latest trend for Italian bars and cafés in town and country, in large cities and villages, is to offer '*primi* first' dishes at moderate

Unconcerned with modern life, a gypsy woman sews in front of Castel S. Angelo in Rome.

prices. Many establishments have posted 'menu *turistico* all included' but also now 'light lunch all included'.

SEEING THE SIGHTS

In Rome you'll want to see Castel S. Angelo, St Peter's, the Sistine Chapel, the Vatican museum, the Borgia apartments and Trastevere—all more or less in the same area. The other places not to be missed are Piazza Venezia, the Campidoglio, the Colosseum and the Palatinate which are in another area. So your sightseeing needs to be planned.

To hire a limousine would be a nice way of doing it. But limos have to cope with the traffic like everyone else. For a modest charge, the Circolare Destra or Circolare Sinistra buses will give you a grand tour of the city, clockwise or anti-clockwise, with the option of getting off wherever you choose. But even though buses have special lanes of their own, they also encounter traffic problems and should be avoided at rush hours.

So let's face it, the best way to see Rome is on foot, one area at a time. You can always hop into a taxi or subside into a neighbouring *trattoria* when you are tired.

This town square is typical of many found throughout Italy.

Filling Up

Since petrol stations are only permitted to open for eight hours a day, most of them close between 12.30 pm and 2.30 pm, and again after 7.30 pm. Those on the *autostrada* network are open at all hours, but motorists driving round the countryside would be well advised to keep their tanks topped up, although some have self-service pumps which accept paper money. There's nothing more annoying than a winking petrol gauge at 12.31 pm with no chance of a refuel.

In Florence, in fact, there's no other way of seeing the sights, because traffic is now banned from most of the *centro storico*. The same goes for cities like Siena and Perugia. (In Venice, of course, there are no wheels at all.)

It's no great hardship even if, as Mary McCarthy observed, the stones of Florence are the hardest to walk on in the world. Sit at a café in the Piazza Signoria and you'll find that three of the greatest art collections in Europe—the Uffizi, the Palazzo Vecchio and the Bargello—are only a few steps away. And the Palazzo Pitti is just across the Ponte Vecchio.

Only on foot can you begin to appreciate the magic of these ancient cities and what Henry James called 'the fusion of human history and moral passion with elements of colour composition and form, that constitute their appeal and give it a supreme, heroic grace'.

So make sure you bring some comfortable shoes. Or buy them on arrival: Italian shoes enjoy a worldwide reputation, in spite of the recent invasion of inexpensive shoes made in Asia.

CLOSING TIMES

A quick snack may be necessary if you're seeing the sights, because most museums are open only until about 2:00 pm. As their time-tables vary from town to town and from season to season, it's difficult to be specific about when is the best time to visit them. One thing is certain: they are nearly all closed on Mondays.

The same early closing business hours apply to post offices, banks, government offices and even ACI (Automobile Club of Italy) offices which only operate in the morning, except in the larger cities, and usually only from Monday to Friday. So make sure you've changed your travellers' cheques before the weekend if you happen to be going into the country. Of course most hotels will take them (at a lower rate) and nowadays will also accept credit cards (though not all of them), but restaurants may not be so amenable, especially in the smaller places.

All cities now have self-service petrol stations operating with paper money, and almost everywhere credit cards and bancomats.

TELEPHONES

The post offices deal with a lot of bureaucratic affairs along with the post, but they don't usually offer telephone facilities. Only those in the major cities do. To put through a call you should look for a telephone kiosk, or better still, go to a bar. Most of them have a circular dialling sign outside, and are equipped with push-button phones. This does away with the tiresome business of inserting *gettoni* (tokens), or even a telephone card, enabling you to make IDD calls without any trouble. You just pay at the end, according to the number of *scatti* (units) employed. As they make a profit on the *scatti*, there's no need to order a drink, though this helps if you want to make a number of calls.

The 'T' sign above the awning of this typical mountain café indicates that cigarettes and stamps are for sale.

Likewise, to buy stamps you don't have to go to a post office. Just look for a blue 'T' sign which indicates a tobacconist's shop. These *tabaccaios* as they are called do more than sell cigarettes. Tobacco being a state monopoly, they also supply other official items such as government forms (*carta bollata*) and stamps, and you'll find a post box on the wall outside. Telephone cards can be bought at most tobacconists or newsagents, also at post offices.

Moreover, it is now possible to send and receive faxes at the post office. If not, they'll tell you where to go for fax and e-mail facilities.

CONVENIENCES

Regrettably, toilet facilities are often a problem. In the big cities there are well-equipped daytime hotels called *Diurno*, usually at the railway station, where you can take a bath or a shower and get everything else you may need, including a haircut. Elsewhere there are WCs (pronounced *vay-chay*, or ask for *toilette*) but they always seem to be tucked away in the most unlikely spots. The bar may have one but not always. However. they'll tell you where to go. Service stations, too. Lately some metal contrivances where you put in a 50 cent or 1 euro coin and the door slides open have begun to appear, but they are still few and far between. If all else fails, stride purposefully into the biggest hotel or café and order a drink afterwards—though that probably won't be necessary.

DRESS

What clothes you wear in town is entirely up to you, and depends on the weather to a large extent. For sightseeing on warm days you certainly don't want to be too buttoned up, and need comfortable shoes. On the other hand you wouldn't expect to go into a smart restaurant in a singlet and shorts, and certainly not into a church—in fact women are expected to wear long sleeves and some

Italian Style

The women look like fashion plates from *Vogue*, even if they are students, low-paid typists or shop assistants (you can spot the rich ones by their display of Bulgari or Beltrami) while the men wear silk suits and look as though they have just come from St Moritz.

sort of hat when they enter a religious establishment if a religious function is being performed. (The rules are posted at the door.)

SMOKING

You may wonder about smoking too. Since 2005, the Sirchia Law forbids smoking in all public places, working places, trains, aeroplanes, bars and cafés, film theatres, buses, public and private offices, schools, universities and public transportation. No more train compartments are reserved for smokers. Some restaurants and cafés may have areas reserved for smokers, usually outside.

A Smoking Culture

Many Italians are inveterate smokers (one has only to recall the pandemonium that ensued when the tobacco workers went on strike in November 1992 and the country ran out of cigarettes: murder was allegedly committed for a carton of cigarettes) so it is unlikely that the anti-smoking lobby will achieve complete success. But you never know!

QUENCHING YOUR THIRST

On the other hand, Italians are very moderate drinkers. There is little insobriety and you'll rarely come across a drunkard, because Italians normally don't touch alcohol on an empty stomach.

True, they may polish off a bottle of wine with their meals, but they would not be indulging in cocktails beforehand. And the oil in the food helps to counteract the effects of the alcohol.

Italian licensing laws are relaxed, which means that people can take their time over a drink. One of the pleasures of Italy is that the bars seem to be open at all hours of the day, and you can wash the dust off your throat whenever you wish.

On many trains, a trolley is brought along with wine, beer and ham rolls. On the *autostradas* there are refreshment bars or restaurants at every service stop. Even the most modest ones contain an imposing array of bottles, including numerous

Hello Italy! At the Piano Grande, high up in the Central Apennines, horticultural art has produced a map of Italy on the bare mountain side.

brands of whisky. This often comes as a surprise to visitors from countries where drinking when driving is regarded as a crime. Legally it is in Italy, too. As for breathalysers, these have been introduced under EU regulations, in Italy like in the rest of Europe. So get to know your limit and don't drink and drive.

The secret is that Italy doesn't have a drink problem. To be under the influence of alcohol is definitely *brutta figura*, a thing to be avoided at all cost. Which Italians do.

TOURING

Once you've found your bearings you'll start wondering what is the best way to get around the country.

Magnificent motorways follow the coastlines and the Autostrada del Sole runs slap down the centre of the country: you can drive from Rome to Milan in not much over five hours, from Bari to Ventimiglia in little over ten hours, and—if you don't mind a long haul—it is possible to cover the whole peninsula in a day's motoring, leaving Brenner at dawn and reaching Sicily in time for a late dinner.

The railway network is equally impressive. Crack trains reach the above destinations in just about the same time, and local ones stop at almost every station.

The choice is yours. It largely depends on the time at your disposal and whether you are travelling alone or with others. Also whether you plan to do the traditional 'Grand Tour' (taking in Florence, Rome, Naples and Venice) or set out on a 'minor tour'—of the Dolomites and the Veneto, for instance.

If you are intending to hop from city to city, there's no doubt that the best bet is to go by train. It will take you right to the city centre and avoid the appalling traffic problems. Most Italians do this nowadays. The railways are efficient and relatively cheap. Since a first-class ticket costs no more and usually much less than the motorway toll to the same destination, let alone the bill for fuel, it's no wonder they leave their cars at home.

For meandering around the countryside you can use the local trains and buses. You can even, if so inclined, hire a bicycle and see nature at close quarters, especially up the hills. (Droves of perspiring cyclists make their way through the steep vineyards of Chianti.) But for mobility and sheer enjoyment, a car is the answer. Indeed for family groups, it is essential.

You can hire one at the airport, or make a leasing arrangement if you are staying long enough. What motoring in Italy involves will be dealt with in detail later on.

THE LAND
AND ITS HISTORY

CHAPTER 2

'A man who has not been in Italy
is always conscious of an inferiority,
from not having seen what it is expected a man should see.'
—Samuel Johnson

GEOGRAPHY

You will probably reach Italy by car or by train, or at one of the regional airports. In fact most of your time is likely to be spent in just one or two regions with side trips, perhaps, to see the sights elsewhere.

There are 20 administrative regions, each of which is autonomous, yet dependent on the central government in Rome. This means that such things as local taxes and regulations, as well as the everyday ways of life, tend to vary from one area to another. As each region has its own separate history and cultural background, you'll soon find that there are considerable differences between them. Sometimes you will almost feel like you have moved into a different land.

So before doing anything else we'll take a quick look at each region, starting at the north. Since Liguria, Piedmont, Lombardy and the two Venezias (along with Trentino-Alto Adige and Aosta) are the only regions to border with other countries, you are bound to find yourself in one of them if you come by land. Nowadays the frontier crossings between Italy and France as well as those with Austria are open. But the usual customs checks remain at the borders of Switzerland and Slovenia, which are not part of the EU.

Liguria

Neighbouring the French Côte d'Azur, Liguria has a famous coastline of its own, shaped like a boomerang, with Genoa in the middle. The western part, which starts at Ventimiglia, is appropriately known as the Riviera dei Fiori, for lining the slopes of the Maritime Alps are thousands of greenhouses that export roses, carnations, irises and other flowers by air and by rail.

Deep valleys cut into the mountains and medieval villages dot the hill tops behind the *autostrada*, the railway and the tourist-packed beaches. After Genoa, the largest port and possibly the least publicised centre in the country—a pity, because it is an old and colourful city with an airport built over the water—comes the Riviera di Levante.

Here the coastline is more rugged, but the vegetation is more luxuriant, full of oleanders, mimosas, olive groves, terraced vines and chestnut woods. Palms line the streets of Rapallo and Levanto, yachts cram the picturesque harbours of Santa Margherita and Portofino, and you'll be struck by the bright colours of the houses painted in every shade of yellow, green, blue, Pompeii red and burned sienna. But inevitably (how else could it have been done?) both railway and *autostrada* are frequently forced underground. All that can be seen from them are the inside of tunnels and rapid flashes of small towns by the sea.

Piedmont

Piedmont lies to the extreme northwest of the country. Since it extends as far as Lake Maggiore, it is the first view you will get of Italy if you come through Simplon (Sempione in Italian).

Set in a curve of the Alps, the regional capital, Turin, once the seat of the Italian royal family, is now the car design centre of Europe and the headquarters of Fiat. A serene metropolis which still retains a strong French influence, it boasts a world-class Automobile Museum which contains over 400 vintage models, and its Egyptology Museum is second only to Cairo's.

In the foothills, rye and barley are grown in large quantities

Rice Production

Out in the countryside, rice is the main crop. Novara and Vercelli produce most of the country's needs (American President Jefferson smuggled some of it out of Piedmont when he was there).

and thousands of cattle yield rich milk and cheese. Around Monferrato some excellent wine is produced, notably sparkling Spumante and velvety Barolo; the viniculture of Piedmont has a long tradition.

Valle D'Aosta

Set further north, Valle d'Aosta might seem at first glance to be part of Piedmont. But no, it is a region in its own right, with even closer associations with France—indeed French ranks as an official language here.

Straddling the picturesquely named Dora Baltea River, Aosta is the biggest valley in that part of Italy. Fifty miles long, it is also one of the most spectacular, being flanked by the Mont Blanc, the Monte Rosa and the Matterhorn peaks, and is guarded by a succession of grimly romantic castles.

Aosta is connected to Switzerland by the Great St Bernard Pass (brandy-toting dogs and a famous hospice), and to France by the Little St Bernard Pass and the seven-mile-long tunnel under the Mont Blanc from Chamonix.

Lombardy

Just to the east of Valle d'Aosta is the richest, most industrialised and populous northern region, Lombardy. Its capital, Milan, is the commercial focal point and main communications centre of Italy.

Milan's huge railway station is almost as famous as its pinnacled and bestatued cathedral, which took four centuries to build. The city is also the home of La Scala Opera Theatre and Leonardo da Vinci's Last Supper fresco, not to mention the international jet-setters and artists who live in the city to make money and enjoy the fast life. Stendhal considered it 'beastly' but loved it all the same. 'Una brutta simpatica,' say partisans and you may agree, though not when you're stuck in a traffic jam.

Longobardi invaders from the north gave Lombardy its name before the Middle Ages, and Lombards have been bankers and businessmen for a millennium. They make everything from engineering products in Bergamo and Brescia to furniture in the Brianza area, silk in Como, violins

Italy is famous for its stunning historical architecture.

in Cremona and sewing machines in Pavia (the ancient Lombard kingdom capital).

The River Po marks Lombardy's southern border and an intricate system of irrigation has stimulated agriculture in the region's flat plains. The region also boasts a thriving dairy industry that makes a score of famous cheeses, among them Gorgonzola and Bel Paese.

To the north Lombardy extends as far as the Alps, coming (at Chiavenna and Sondrio) to within skiing distance of St Moritz. Lake Maggiore and Lake Garda demarcate the western and eastern boundaries. Lake Como with its palatial villas is just to the east of Lake Maggiore.

Trentino-Alto Adige

This region covers most of the Dolomites, one of the loveliest parts of Europe, and includes the Brenner Pass which has always been the easiest and chief highway across the Alps.

Until early last century, the region was part of the Austro-Hungarian Empire which then reached the southern tip of Lake Garda and bordered with Lombardy to the west and Venezia to the east. But after World War I things changed. The 1919 Treaty of Versailles gave this territory to Italy and it became the new region of Trentino-Alto Adige—the Adige being the river that runs down from the Brenner.

All very complicated—especially for the southern Tirolians, many of whom, still rooted in their Austrian and German culture, have maintained a strong degree of autonomy. You will find, for instance, that they still speak German there.

Territory
In 1919, Italy was given sovereignty over Trieste as well as the neighbouring peninsula of Istria, which later became part of Yugoslavia after World War II.

The Veneto

Circumscribing the great lagoon which contains Venice and its islands, the Veneto embraces the mouth of the Po and stretches inland as far as the border with Lombardy. The landscape surrounding Venice tends to be flat and desolate where the sea has receded; elsewhere it is covered by a crescendo urban sprawl. But there are some lovely neo-classic villas by Palladio along the banks of the Brenta and extensive vineyards behind Verona which, like Padua and Vicenza, forms part of the Veneto.

As for Venice itself, which has been called an absurd and wonderful dream—'a kind of poem in stone accidentally written by history on the waters'—what can one say? To quote Henry James, it is a great pleasure to write the word, but there is a certain impudence in pretending to add anything to it.

Fruili-Venezia Giulia

Friuli-Venezia Giulia runs eastwards along the bay of the Adriatic to Trieste (the gate to Central Europe that James Joyce loved so much) and northwards to Austria and Slovenia in the Carnac Alps. Agriculture, especially orchards and vineyards producing the famous *grappa*, predominates in the Friuli. There is a good deal of light industry around Pordenone, and plenty of tourist establishments along the Adriatic.

Emilia-Romagna

Drive down the Autostrada del Sole ('The Freeway of Sunshine') and from Piacenza onwards you are in Emilia—named after Marcus Aemilius Lepidus, who built the great Roman road leading straight through Parma (opera, cheese and ham), Modena (pigs' trotters, sparkling Lambrusco wine, Ferrari cars) and Bologna (crooked towers, ancient university and gastronomy).

Bologna is the capital of this double-barrelled region; south of the city you are in Romagna and pass through Imola (motor-racing circuit), Faenza (ceramics), Forli (furniture), Cesena (Cesare Borgia's lair) to reach Rimini, half-seriously dubbed 'the Las Vegas of Italy' by its inhabitants and the birthplace of Fellini. A few miles up the coast is Ravenna, the former capital of the Western Roman Empire, and celebrated for its early Christian mosaics, their golden backgrounds showing the influence of the Orient on Italian art.

Emilia-Romagna marks the southern limit of what is regarded as Northern Italy. We now reach Central Italy and move into Tuscany.

Tuscany

To many people Tuscany is the most fascinating part of the country. Once the home of the Etruscans (whose enigmatic smiles still seem to appear from time to time on modern Tuscan faces) and birthplace of the Renaissance, Tuscany is the balancing point of Italy, a harmonised blending of north and south.

The scenery ranges from snowy peaks and rolling foothills to lovingly tended farms and dolce vita beaches. Yet the landscape—half-wooded, half-cultivated—has an equilibrium derived from its basic mineral elements: stone, clay and marble. And as if culture were mapping nature without disrupting its quality, the towns display the materials the land is made of.

Castellina in Chianti is a favourite tourist destination in Tuscany. This street lies behind the historic ramparts and most houses here date from the 15th and 16th centuries.

Florence

In Florence, a city of magnificently sculpted stones, the buildings seem to emerge from slabs of raw rock, becoming more and more polished as they reach the upper floors. Strong, severe, but always aesthetic and inspiring, this is unmistakably the architecture of Italy's cultural centre. In no other place are so many masterpieces crammed into so small an area.

Siena

And what about Siena? It must be the last medieval city in Europe. With its forest-clad hills and its winding green valleys, Tuscany is like a park in which each knoll is crowned by an ancient village, a *castello* or a church. Framed by cypresses, olive groves or vineyards, and bathed in luminosity, every view has the quality of a *trecento* painting. To travel through the Tuscan countryside (and taste its famous wines) is a continuous delight.

Umbria

As you move west into Umbria the light changes, turning greener as olive groves and thicker woods take the place of vineyards, and the stone becomes more pink. Umbria is often called Tuscany's little sister or the green heart of Italy, perhaps because it is the only region which is entirely inland. The Tiber runs slap through Terni at the centre, and Lake Trasimeno (on the shores of which Hannibal routed the Romans in 217 BC) has a silvery, dream-like aura.

The capital, Perugia, whose blood-stained history was dominated in the Renaissance by the Baglioni dynasty, is both a centre of learning and an industrial complex. Todi, a medieval gem, is surrounded by the remains of Etruscan and Roman walls. Gubbio is grimmer, lorded over by the lofty 14th-century Palazzo dei Consoli.

The Marche

Lying on the Adriatic slopes of the Apennines south of Romagna, the Marche sports a

Assisi

Assisi, where St Francis was born, remains a serene and spiritual vision of the Middle Ages.

Originally inhabited by the Piceni tribes, the region was colonised by Rome (the civil wars started at Ascoli in 90 BC) and later became part of the Papal States. As it formed the *marca* (border) of their empire, the Germans called this region the Marca of Ancona, from which the name is derived.

hundred-mile coastline which runs almost straight from the tiny independent state of San Marino (the oldest republic in Europe) to Ascoli Piceno.

Though the sandy beaches are lined with tourist resorts backed by hundreds of small factories, the interior is unspoilt. Most of the region is hilly and in the uplands an arpeggio of hill towns, perched on every crag, lends an operatic quality. After all, this is Rossini land.

The landscape is a patchwork of closely-worked fields and woods. Sheltered by the Apennines, this is a lovely hidden land, largely unknown to the outside world (though the British seem to have discovered its charms recently) apart from celebrated places of artistic and religious pilgrimage such as Urbino and Loreto.

Abruzzi and Molise

Two autonomous regions that are traditionally linked together, Abruzzi and Molise cover the highest part of the Apennines

The Marche hillside provides a conducive environment for writers and historians alike.

south of the Marche. It is wild but beautiful country, partly a national park; the climate is rugged with frost in the mountains except in high summer. There is a certain amount of agriculture in sheltered valleys and some industry around the capital, Pescara, which is a busy fishing port.

Visitors come to bathe in the Adriatic or ski on the Gran Sasso, and also to enjoy the remains of the old way of life of the shepherds.

We are now well into the Mezzogiorno, that is to say the southern part of Italy. Here the climate is noticeably warmer, and the people have a more Mediterranean look about them. Their behaviour is different and you sense a change in the way of life as you cross into Apulia.

Apulia

This elongated region stretches along the Adriatic coast from the Gargano promontory—a sort of mountainous spur on the boot of Italy—down to the heel of the peninsula.

This is the largest southern region and it has the widest plain between the Apennines and the sea. The flat land provides a livelihood for over half the inhabitants who cultivate wheat, vegetables and fruit as well as the ubiquitous olive (some of the gnarled trees are centuries old) and the vineyards that produce the strong Apulian wine. Tobacco is grown too.

It is rocky terrain, marked by endless stone walls which have been built less to divide the fields than to clear the soil. Apart from large villas at the centre of the big estates, there are surprisingly few farmhouses to be seen. In the past, the farmers have always congregated in highly populated villages, often far from their work, for security reasons. Many of the towns, such as Lucera, have imposing castles (mostly put up by Emperor Frederick II Hohenstaufen) and magnificent Romanesque cathedrals like those at Trani and Molfetta, two delightful fishing ports to the north of the regional capital, Bari.

Prehistoric Remains

Around Alberobello you will find the famous *trulli*—groups of beehive-shaped houses built of dry-stone in a design that goes back to prehistoric times.

Bari was a great port in the days of the Crusades, and it has developed since World War II into an important industrial centre. Further down the coast, Brindisi, traditionally the end of the Appian Way, continues to be the gateway to Greece, while on the other side of the gulf Taranto is a flourishing naval port and dockyard.

Basilicata

Westwards along the instep of the boot, so to speak, is the smallest southern region, Basilicata. Apart from a short and rather dull coastline it is nearly all mountainous. Potenza, the chief city, is 3000 feet above sea level and reputed to have the coldest climate in Italy in winter.

Wild, rocky and forested, this is a world apart. Its villages are relics of the Middle Ages (in Matera there are still some cave dwellings) and its agriculture for the most part is hardly above subsistence level. Things are improving, to be sure —there are big development schemes in progress—but even so life remains a battle for survival.

Calabria

Standing on the toe of Italy, Calabria is equally mountainous. Aspromonte is over 7000 feet high, and the Silagian plateau not much less. Yet a few miles from these sweeping upland pastures, from emerald lakes and deep forests, there curls an almost tropical-looking shoreline covered with citrus trees and olive groves, not to mention an unending string of garish holiday resorts.

The difference in climate is striking: Norman Douglas wrote that he had been colder up in the mountains than he could ever recall, while down by the sea people were bathing. This contrast is said to be reflected in the character of the inhabitants. Though Calabrians are usually cheerful and easy-going, they can also be feckless.

Fifty years ago, much of the region was malarial. You had to hurry indoors before sunset and there was hardly anywhere to stay. Nowadays, you will be well looked after in a network of hotels and motels, restaurants and petrol stations. Moreover you'll find that the people are friendly in a rather old-fashioned way.

Campania

To the north of Calabria, Campania presents a different scene again. This is the richest region of southern Italy and also the most colourful with its blue skies, oranges, tomatoes, peppers, corn fields, olive groves and vine-festooned trees.

The bay of Naples has a legendary half-moon perfection. The islands of Capri and Ischia emerge from an iridescent sea. Vesuvius occasionally gently smokes, Amalfi and Positano are picturesquely perched on the wooded Sorrento peninsula.

Naples

The heart of Campania is Naples with its harlequins at every street corner and urchins darting through alleys festooned with washing lines (mind your wallet!). It's a bustling, noisy, baroque and joyous city, for despite all the hardships, Neapolitans always manage to come up with a grin. Their secret is to have perfected *l'arte di arrangiarsi*, which means the art of getting by. They are Mr and Mrs Fixits. But don't miss their zest for life and their extraordinary human quality.

Moreover the pressures of modern life have added to the Neapolitans' fondness for playing creative and amusing tricks and some more sinister activities. As a result, Naples has acquired the reputation of being a tough and sometimes dangerous place, one to visit with caution.

Lazio

Lazio (Latium in English) got its name from the Latini tribe who lived there even before Rome was founded. This region stretches northwards from the Gulf of Gaeta to the Tuscan maremma, and from south of Umbria along the Apennines to Molise.

A mosaic of different colours and textures, Lazio possesses few mineral riches. The coastline is so sandy that Civitavecchia is the only port that has not silted up; below the volcanic Alban hills stretches the huge flat expanse of the Campagna di Roma, until recently a death-trap for malaria

Step Back in Time

In the Campania region, at Pompeii and Herculaneum, you can see how the ancient Romans lived.

and still inhabited mainly by shepherds. And yet, surprisingly, this desolate landscape was the cradle of ancient Rome.

Rome

Rome is surrounded by magnificent buildings—Castelgandolfo, Frascati, Tivoli, the Villa Adriana, the monastery of Grottaferrata, to name but a few—but it is the Eternal City that dominates the scene. For the visitor, Lazio means Rome.

The largest metropolis in Italy, Rome is the seat of government, of the Papacy, of the whole labyrinthine machine of Italian bureaucracy. Rome is full of civil servants, diplomats and clerics, but above all of incomparable treasures and so harmonious an architecture that the buildings of two millennia blend happily side by side.

From the Senate which governs today's republic can be seen the ruins of the edifices that ran the Roman Empire. The railway station incorporates a portion of the Roman city walls, St Peter's is the biggest church in the world, the Castel S. Angelo, a stronghold around which so much of the city's history is centred, was originally built as Hadrian's mausoleum, and so on. Immersed in the everyday life of Rome are more antiques and more art than anywhere else in the world.

A feast to the eye, to the senses. On his first day in Rome in 1869, Henry James wrote: 'At last, for the first time, I live.' Alas, cars and their exhausts have wiped out much of the old romance. Nowadays you can scarcely move around, hardly even breathe. The traffic is so chaotic that Romans, it is said, frequently nip off for an espresso while their cars are stuck in the jam.

Even so there are plenty of pleasures to be enjoyed, if you're prepared to put up with the frustrations.

That completes our thumbnail sketches of peninsular Italy. But we must not forget the two islands off the coast.

Sicily

The largest and most beautiful of all the Mediterranean islands, Sicily lies like a baroque concert grand dumped at the toe of Italy.

Founded by the Phoenicians, colonised by the Greeks, conquered by the Romans, taken over successively by the Arabs, the Normans, the French (very briefly), the Spanish and finally ruled by the Bourbons until Garibaldi brought deliverance in 1860, Sicily has survived a number of culture shocks.

What emerged was an architecture in which Saracen-Christian, Spanish Gothic and flamboyant rococo have been combined into a mixture that is pungently and recognisably Sicilian. It is also a land of such splendid Greek temples that the saying goes: 'If you want to see Greece, come to Sicily.'

From Theocritus of Syracuse to Verga (Cavalleria Rusticana), Lampedusa and Pirandello, Sicily has produced a whole host of writers who have chronicled its charms and given the universal message of this fascinating yet disturbing island.

A Sicilian Tour

Sicily is a tapestry in which the whole exuberant Mediterranean way of life is enacted in front of your eyes. Don't miss the chance to do a round tour of the island if the opportunity occurs.

Sardinia

Although geographically close to Sicily, Sardinia is quite different. Until quite recent times, it has remained isolated, even from the mainland.

The majority of Sardinians are shepherds, proud of their island and afraid of the sea, it is commonly said, because that was where trouble came from. If they had any historical contacts, it was with Catalonia (Barcelona) in Spain. Even today their culture and language are less contaminated with outside influences than those of any other Italian region.

The people appear sober and rugged like the interior of the island, and their cuisine owes nothing to the sea. Only in the last 50 years have the beautiful beaches of the Costa Smeralda been developed for international tourism.

HISTORY

The history of Italy spans 3000 years and can be written at any magnitude. Indeed, the authors have condensed it

Throughout Italy, you can still find properties which date back hundreds of years.

into a single small volume *(Italy: a Travel History)* and have also written more comprehensive histories of Tuscany and the Marche. Yet the themes are so involved, the action so complicated, the events so dramatic, that a thumbnail sketch is virtually impossible. It would not even scratch the surface.

So here is a chronology:

- 1000 BC   Start of the Iron Age and Villanovan culture

- 735 BC   Traditional date of the founding of Rome

- 509 BC   The expulsion of the Tarquins ends Etruscan control of Rome and the Republic begins

- 450 BC   Roman laws are codified

- 264 BC   Start of the Punic Wars between Rome and Carthage which made Rome mistress of the western Mediterranean and ended (in 146 BC) with Carthage's destruction

- 106 BC   Birth of Cicero, Rome's greatest orator and a leading figure in the last decades of the Republic

- 73 BC   Rebellion of the Slaves led by Spartacus

- 70 BC   Birth of the poet Virgil

- 44 BC   Assassination of Julius Caesar by an aristocratic conspiracy headed by Brutus and Cassius

- 32 BC   War against Mark Antony and Cleopatra, Queen of Egypt

- 27 BC   Augustus (formerly Octavian) becomes the first Roman emperor and establishes the Roman imperial system

- AD 193   The year of the four emperors: Didius Julianus wins the throne by offering the largest donation to the praetorian guard, but by the end of the year Septimius Severus is proclaimed emperor by the army and founds the Severan dynasty

- 313   The Edict of Milan abolishes religious discrimination and marks the triumph of Christianity over persecution

- 330   Constantinople (ancient Byzantium) becomes the capital of the empire and identifies with a new Roman-Christian civilisation

- 380   Christianity becomes the sole official state religion and other cults are proscribed

- 402   Barbarian invasions: sack of Rome by the Visigoths in 410

- 476   Fall of the Roman Empire in the west. Imperial Rome gradually replaced by Papal Rome

- 568   The Lombard invasion of Italy

- 800–600   Etruscan dominance in central Italy and the 'Homeric age' of Magna Grecia in the south

- 800   Charlemagne, king of the Franks, who championed the Church against the Lombards, crowned as emperor by Pope Leo III

- 952   Italy becomes a German fief and part of the Holy Roman Empire

- 1097   The First Crusade. Godfrey of Bouillon captures Jerusalem

- 1176   Emperor Frederick I defeated at the battle of Legnano by an army of the Lombard League. The Lombard cities agree to recognise the emperor as their overlord, but their right to govern themselves is safeguarded by the Peace of Constance (1183)

- 1181   Birth of St Francis of Assisi, founder of the Franciscan Order

- 1194   Birth at Iesi of Emperor Frederick II who was brought up in Sicily and lived chiefly in southern Italy, regarding Germany as merely a source of men and money for his incessant wars against the Papacy. Known as 'Stupor Mondi' he was a poet and scientist in the centre of a brilliant court. He founded Naples University in 1225 and the first school of poetry in Italy

- 1200   The population of Italy numbers about 8.5 million

- 1265   Birth of Dante Alighieri

- 1273   Gold ducats coined in Venice. Start of the Venetian Empire.

- 1300   The first Holy Year. Change of climatic conditions in Europe which experiences a colder phase until 1800, punctuated by a warmer period in the 16th century. Population of Italy is 11 million

- 1348   Outbreak of the Black Death, reducing the population to about 8 million

- 1377   Birth of Brunelleschi

- 1434   Banker Cosimo de' Medici founds a dynasty that ruled Florence and later Tuscany (with no formal title) until 1737. A patron of scholars and artists, he was associated with many of the enterprises that made Florence the leader of Renaissance Italy

- 1469   Lorenzo de' Medici becomes the third member of his family to rule Florence at a period of great progress in the arts and in learning

Clearly visible at the foot of this stone wall on the Piazza Michaelangelo, Florence is the shadow of David, the famous statue which was carved from a single piece of marble by Michaelangelo at the age of 29.

- 1492   Christopher Columbus, the Genoese navigator-explorer, becomes the first European to reach America

- 1501   War between Spain and France for possession of Naples, which ended up under Spanish control in 1504

- 1520   Leo X issues a papal bull condemning Martin Luther as a heretic for his 41 propositions; Luther burns it publicly at Wittenberg. Protestantism is established and the Reformation begins

- 1530   Charles V crowned by the Pope as Emperor and King of Italy

- 1545–63   The Council of Trent, held to fix the doctrinal differences between Catholics and Protestants, results in the Counter-Reformation and the notorious Inquisition

- 1612–17   First war between Spain and Savoy for the Monferrato region

- 1630   Milan badly hit by an outbreak of the plague in northern Italy

- 1704   French troops invade Piedmont and are chased out by the Austrians who take their place

- 1733   The first masonic lodge founded in Florence

- 1735   Italy's oldest newspaper, *La Gazzetta di Parma*, begins publication

- 1762   The so-called Villa dei Papiri unearthed at Herculaneum

- 1796   Napoleon's Italian campaign. Piedmont surrenders Savoy and Nice to France, and after its victory over the Austrians, France takes possession of Lombardy and the Romagna and sets up the Venetian Republic. Subsequently, by the Treaty of Campoformio, Napoleon exchanges the Veneto and Istria with Austria against recognition of his annexation of Belgium and the extension of France's frontier to the Rhine

- 1805   Having transformed the Italian republic into a monarchy, Napoleon is crowned King of Italy in Milan

- 1806   Napoleon's brother made king of Naples

- 1815   After the collapse of the Napoleonic empire, the Congress of Vienna restores the status quo in Italy

- 1848   First war of independence against Austria

- 1859   Second war of independence. With the help of Napoleon III, the Austrians are repulsed. Lombardy is clawed back, and after a plebiscite Tuscany and Romagna join the kingdom of Savoy

- 1860   At the head of 1000 red-shirted irregulars, Garibaldi defeats the kingdoms of Naples and Sicily and becomes a legend in his lifetime. Pledging the support of the *mezzogiorno*, he salutes Victor Emmanuel as king of Italy

- 1861   Further plebiscites bring Umbria and the Marche into the fold and on 17 March the first Italian Parliament proclaims the country to be a constitutional monarchy with Victor Emmanuel as sovereign

- 1865   The capital of Italy transferred from Turin to Florence

- 1870   Venice finally wrested from Austria and the Italian army enters Rome through a breach in the Porta Pia

- 1871   Rome once again the capital of a united Italy, and the Papacy finds its powers relegated to spiritual matters

- 1882   Following the widening of electoral suffrage —from 600,000 to 2 million—the left gains ground and the first socialist deputy elected

- 1889   Italy colonises Somalia

- 1895   Unsuccessful war with Ethiopia, but Italy occupies Eritrea

- 1901   General census sets the population at 33,778,000

- 1909   Socialist gains at the elections and entry into parliament of 'Catholic deputies', one of whom, being a priest, is excommunicated by the Pope

- 1912   Universal suffrage for all males over the age of 21 who can read and write, increasing the number of voters to over 8 million

- 1915   Italy enters World War I on the side of the Allies

- 1919   The Italian delegation walks out of the Versailles Peace Conference over the question of Fiume, and D'Annunzio occupies the city with a band of volunteers

- 1921   The Italian Communist Party is formed under the leadership of Gramsci

- 1922   Following the march on Rome by Mussolini's Fascists, King Victor Emmanuel III asks Mussolini to form a new government

- 1925   Mussolini assumes dictatorial powers, and subsequently dissolves the political parties. The opposition is muzzled and Gramsci is condemned to life imprisonment (1928)

- 1929   Lateran Pact between Mussolini and Cardinal Gasparri which ends the conflict between Church and State. The Vatican State is established and Catholicism becomes the state religion, taught in all schools

- 1939   Mussolini occupies Albania

- 1940   Mussolini declares war against France and England

- 1941   Germany and Italy declare war on the USA. The Italian empire is lost. In May this year, the British take Eritrea and Ethiopia, and Hailè Selassiè takes back possession of his throne

- 1943   The Grand Council substitutes Marshal Badoglio in the place of Mussolini, who is arrested but rescued by German paratroops and founds a socialist counter-government at Salo on Lake Garda, which is controlled by the Germans. Badoglio declares war on Germany. US and British force land in Sicily

- 1944   Allied armies land at Anzio and push the Germans north

- 1945   Mussolini attempts to flee disguised as a German soldier but is caught by the partisans and executed

- 1946   Following a national referendum (12,717923 against;10,719,284 for the monarchy) the Republic of Italy is created and King Umberto II goes into exile

- 1948   The electorate gives 48 per cent of its votes to De Gasperi's centre-right government comprising the Christian Democrats and their smaller allies against 30 per cent for the Communists and Socialists

- 1955   Italy is admitted to UNO

- 1960   The 'Italian miracle': in 10 years, the GNP has increased by 47 per cent

- 1978   Christian Democrats' president Aldo Moro is kidnapped and murdered by the Red Brigades

- 1981   Coalition government headed by Spadolini, the first non Christian Democrat prime minister since the formation of the Republic. Census shows that population is now 56,566,991

- 1984   New concordat between State and Church

- 1986   Socialist Craxi's administration resigns after
             1000 days, thus far the longest spell in power
             of any post-war government

- 1993   Tangentopoli, the gentle or 'clean
             hands' revolution

- 1998   New law regulating the presence of foreign
             residents. In this period, an estimated
             1,100,000 foreign citizens and an estimated
             350,000 illegal aliens reside in Italy

- 1999   Inauguration of the euro (1 euro =
             1936.27 lire)

- 2001   Berlusconi is elected Prime Minister

- 2003   Foreign residents are 1,990,159 (Data
             from ISTAT Government Office for
             Statistics). Illegal aliens are estimated at
             around 500,000

- 2005   Death of John Paul II, elected in 1978

THE ITALIAN PEOPLE

CHAPTER 3

'The traveller who has gone to Italy to study
the tactile values of Giotto, or the corruption of the Papacy,
may return remembering nothing but the blue sky
and the men and women under it.'
—E M Forster

THE FAMILY

The Italian defines himself by his appurtenance to his village, province, region, etc. But first and foremost his loyalty is to his family.

Derived directly from the ancient Roman *gens* (clan), the modern Italian family forms the backbone of Italy's culture today. The permanence and equilibrium provided by family ties explain what would otherwise seem a baffling paradox: namely, how it is possible for such a diversified collection of regions—'a thrown together bunch of republics' as the Renaissance historian Varchi described them—to preserve any unity of culture. And on a political level, how could a nation that has changed its government more than once every year since World War II have remained relatively stable?

The answer to these questions is undoubtedly the stabilising force of the family. The Italian family is a patriarchal family with three, sometimes four, generations living under the same roof and maintaining strong ties with cousins as well as a whole host of kinsfolk. (After all, the Mafia took the 'family' as a model for its solidity and held to it for almost a century.)

Habitually, the patriarchal Italian family was headed by the grandfather who was also the economic leader. His authority passed on to the eldest son, and often the first male grandchild was named after him to emphasise the continuity of the clan. The family lands and occupations tended to pass down the lineage from one generation to another. Younger sons might change professions, but the first-born continued doing what his father and forebears had done. Moreover the heritage laws favoured the first-born and younger sons at the expense of their sisters.

Girls brought a dowry to their husband's patrimony—a term that emphasises the father's substance. However the mother had an analogous power. She oversaw the functioning of the household and the running of the house.

When the children married, they continued to live in the family home. A feature of Italian architecture is the villa divided into flats for the various generations. All over the country there are shops, hotels and enterprises of every sort which are run solely by members of the same family.

The Italian family, however extended, was (and to some extent still is) very close-knit, spending the weekends together and often eating its meals collectively. Unity was its strength.

The Nuclear Family

All this ended in the 1960s when the patriarchal family came to a sudden end, and the nuclear family emerged, creating repercussions that are too fundamental to be assessed at present. It is true that grandparents remain involved acting as outside help to raise the children and that the family links remain strong even if its members are dispersed.

But for the new family, one salary was no longer sufficient. So many women went to work, which gave them greater power and status, even if it often meant double work—at home and on the job. Feminism, which hitherto had been disregarded, was encouraged by the left-wing parties and intellectual circles. Despite Vatican opposition, divorce and abortion were legalised in the 1970s after a nationwide referendum.

For those who like statistics, the present resident population is almost 58 million. Divorce figures are approximately 27.5 million males and half a million females. The number of Italian families in 2003 was over 22 million with their average

In Italy, the child is father of the man. Certainly, little girls are always the focus of attention.

number of members being 2.6. There are many single-parent families too. In 2003, 25.4 per cent of the total number of families were formed by single-parent families. In 1995, that figure was lower at 21.1 per cent. By comparison, nuclear families in 2003 totalled 40.8 per cent. Couples without children were just 19 per cent. Italian legislature recognises the equality of men and women in all fields, though society still remains slightly male-oriented.

And what happened to the 'typical Italian family' consisting of five or more members? In 2003, they were 6.8 per cent of all Italian families. Ten years earlier, they were 8.4 per cent.

FRIENDSHIP

Chi trova un amico trova un tesoro runs the old Italian proverb— 'he who finds a friend finds a treasure'. Another adage says: *Amici a scelta e parenti come sono*, meaning 'choose your friends and accept relatives for what they are'. Both underscore the fact that friends in the true sense of the word are few and rare in Italy, even if it is in the nature of Italians to be friendly and sociable.

A friend is as precious as a member of the family. Friendship involves total support, total acceptance, and total availability. It is something that grows imperceptibly with time and requires continuous proof of affection, even at a distance.

The Art of Friendship

Be aware of the everlasting obligations you take on when you befriend an Italian. Better start by being a good acquaintance—*buona conoscenza*—and gradually move on to become a 'good friend' and finally a 'true friend' with the passage of time.

THE ITALIAN LOVER

The Italian lover, if press reports are to be believed, is not what he used to be. Rossano Brazzi, Marcello Mastroianni and the like have few imitators among the younger generation.

Jet-setting playboys as well as *pappagalli* in the streets and the cafés have allegedly lost their flamboyant style. Social psychologists believe that the basic reason for this is that they have been deprived of their two ideals of femininity—the virgin-mother and the whore-lover. Or in milder terms, the motherly submissive woman and the carefree sensuous companion.

Having to find both in the same contemporary egalitarian woman seems to be the main problem of the Italian male today, along with an increasing obsession with diets and health matters—cholesterol, sugar levels in the blood and so on. But the old habit of paying courteous attention to women survives, and men still jump to their feet when a woman appears, open doors for her and pay the bills.

In a recent issue of *Cosmopolitan* magazine, Avedon and Molli suggested that, considering the adolescent charm of Italian males (their romanticism and their attachment to mama), the best recipe was to love and leave them. Yet recent statistics put the figure of intercultural marriages at more than half a million in Italy.

THE WEIGHT OF TRADITION

Take a look at the Italian calendar and you'll see that certain months are still dedicated to pagan Gods—for instance,

Gennaio (January) is named after Janus; *Marzo* (March) after Mars; May after *Maia;* June after *Juno*, and so forth. So are the days of the week: *Lunedi* is moon day; *Martedi* the day of Mars; *Mercoledi* is the day of Hercules; *Giovedi,* of Jupiter; *Venerdi*, of Venus; *Sabato* (Sabbath) is for the Judeo-Christian God, and *Domenica* (the day of Dominus, the Lord) is Christian.

These names embrace astrology, paganism, Judaic and Christian heritage, mingled side by side. Furthermore the week starts on Monday and ends on Sunday—following the biblical story of the Creation—which is a clear example of how deeply tradition is engraved in Italian culture.

FESTIVALS, SAINTS AND THE YEAR CYCLE

As Christian saints replaced the old pagan gods, they were assigned their own place in the calendar. Each day is given over to one or more patron saint—you'll see their names on most Italian calendars. Christmas replaced the Roman celebrations of the rising sun; Easter and Pentecost, both mobile, were calculated by the moon calendar, which is older than the present sun-based calendar; the Assumption replaced the Roman *Feriae Augusti.*

Saints

The various trades and professions have their specific patron saints, from peasants who venerate St Isidoro to surgeons who pay homage to St Cosma and St Damian. Advertisers have St Bernardino, photographers St Veronica, carpenters St Joseph, motorists St Christopher.

Of course not all Italians venerate saints and there is a great deal of latitude in the way the cult is followed. Yet tradition runs on and these intermediaries between our world and the next continue to receive ex-voto offerings for graces and favours. These may take the form of painted tablets depicting the instance in which the saint is believed to have intervened, or jewelled plaques depicting a limb that has been healed.

Certain saints are accorded a special patronage—St Lucia for the eyes, St Blaise for the throat, St Agatha for women's

Christianity, in particular Roman Catholicism, pervades Italian life. Even in out-of-the-way places, there are beautiful churches to visit.

breasts, St Dominic the Abbot for teeth, St Anthony the Hermit for animals.

Specialist saints have deep local roots. For instance, in Apulia, St Donato is prayed to for epilepsy, St Marco for earaches, St Marina for headaches, St Paolo for dog and tarantula bites, St Pantaleo for carbuncles, St Venanzio for rheumatism, St Rocco for cripples, and St Antonino and St Liberata for people who are thought to be possessed by the devil. Cities, towns and even villages have a patron saint of their own: Milan has St Ambroise, Naples has St Gennaro, Venice has St Mark the Evangelist, Genoa has St George, Palermo has St Rosalia, Florence has St John the Baptist, Assisi has St Francis, Siena has St Catherine, Bari has St Nicholas and so on.

The Year Cycle

Like elsewhere, the year cycle is marked by festivals. First of all there are the solstices and the equinoxes—December, March, June, September—for which the celebrations are archaic and agrarian in origin. Then there are the many Christian feast days which are marked by religious ceremonies and processions, parades, banquets (with blessed or traditional food), games, markets and regattas.

Italians who live in foreign parts will make a point of returning on such occasions to renew their ties with home, links which are still strong and perhaps more important than ever in these days of 'global society'.

Civic pride, religious heritage, the itch for social and territorial identity are cardinal reasons for the Italian love of festivals, many of which have remained unchanged since the days of the Roman Empire or the Renaissance.

In imperial times there were 182 festive days a year. 'Too many heads, too many festivals, too many storms' ran the old proverb, and what remains of this thickly interwoven texture of traditions is briefly as follows:

Festivals

For three centuries now, 1 January has been the official beginning of the year. But in Italian tradition the yearly cycle is marked by the 12-day period between Christmas and Epiphany—the latter being personified by the Befana, an old lady riding a donkey who comes down the chimney on the night of 5 January and brings presents for the children whose stockings have been left in readiness by the fireplace.

That same night the *befani*—kids dressed up as old people—go from door to door wishing everyone a good year and asking for little gifts or tips similar to Halloween in the Anglo-Saxon world. But in Italy this practice is probably a throwback to the ancient ritual of *renovatio temporis* when dead ancestors were honoured with symbolic gifts.

This symbolic exchange of gifts may also lie behind the shopping sprees during the holiday season and the subsequent period of clearance sales in January, which is carnival time.

Carnivals

Carnival time represents a regeneration of energy for the community and nature after a period of chaos. Italian carnivals are the modern counterparts of the Roman Saturnalia—a time of licence and representation of a topsy-turvy world before the return of the golden age. Also of the medieval 'feasts of fools' when sacred places were ritually profaned by masks and obscene chanting, not to mention the Renaissance carnivals in Florence, which were so splendidly staged by the Medicis. (Machiavelli observed that the Medicis' festival policy aimed at keeping the city abundant, the nobility honoured, and the people quiet.)

The same theme recurred during the Baroque age in Rome and the decadent but refined carnivals of Venice at the time of Casanova in the 18th century. Goethe, who participated in the Roman carnivals of 1787 and 1788, regarded them as a metaphor for life itself, where 'freedom and equality can be enjoyed only in the midst of folly'.

Today's carnivals take place just about everywhere. In Venice the city becomes a kaleidoscope of individual masks, beautifully staged against the architecture of the city and mirrored by the waters. In Viareggio and San Remo there are parades of enormous floats inspired by topical themes

such as politics and ecology, peace and war. In Ivrea, a furious battle takes place between groups of youngsters from different parts of the city, with oranges as weapons.

To recapture the spirit of the old agrarian carnivals and their ancient rites of purification one must go to smaller cities, or to villages such as Tufara in the Molise region.

There you find enacted the trial and execution of a figure representing Carnival, which embodies all the public and private sins of the community, jocularly set forth in rhyme. The death of Carnival is staged by burning a huge straw puppet, as Fellini recorded in his haunting film, *Amarcord*.

Midnight on Mardi Gras—*Martedi Grasso*—marks the beginning of Lent, a 40-day period of penance and purification in preparation for Easter. Gone is the pagan flavour of carnival. Yet half-way through Lent there is a brief moment of excitement when the rite of *segalavecchia* (literally, saw-the-old-lady) takes place. A puppet in the shape of an old lady representing Lent is cut in two halves, and from its womb come all sorts of goodies—sweets, sausages and eggs—to celebrate earth's bounty after the long winter season.

Easter

The concept of resurrection after death, common to so many religions, finds its apogee in the liturgy of Easter. But apart from the customary ceremonies on Good Friday, a few medieval rituals still survive, such as the processions of penitents in places like Nocera Tirinese in Calabria or Guardia Sanframondi in Campania, where penitents flagellate themselves or indulge in bloody acts of devotion to acknowledge Christ's sacrifice.

Other spectacles which take place (largely in Sicily) include restaging Christ's entrance into Jerusalem and His journey to Calvary. There is the procession of the Mysteries in Trapani, and a 'dance of the devils' in Prizzi.

Easter Sunday concludes the Holy Week joyfully with decorated Easter eggs containing surprises (the symbols of life) and Easter lamb (the sacrificial animal); the festivities end with the traditional Easter Monday picnic in the country.

Spring

May celebrates nature's revival and many present-day rituals reflect the age-old urge to bestow its new energy on humans themselves. Itinerant serenades known as *cantar maggio* ('to sing May') are performed by youngsters of both sexes, and archaic theatrical shows—the *maggi*—depict epic themes with music and dances. (These are particularly prevalent in the mountains between Tuscany and Emilia.) A King and a Queen of May are elected from among the local youngsters, a custom that foreshadowed, perhaps, the beauty and body-building contests of today.

The Roman goddess Maia not only gave her name to the month, but also to her pet animal, the *maiale* (pig). Later, May became the month of Mary, and because to marry then is supposed to bring good luck, many weddings take place during the month of May.

Italy has many traditions and festivals which take place around the year.

Racing bareback three times round the Campo in Siena's famous *Palio*, medieval rules prevail, with no holds barred.

It is also the season of the 'dancing towers', a ceremony which may well be of pagan origin. In Gubbio, for example, three enormous machines called *ceri* are hauled up the mountain to the basilica of the city's patron saint, the bishop Ubaldo, by hundreds of worshippers.

These forms of devotion, which you'll also find at Viterbo in Lazio and at Nola in Campania, along with the 'wedding of the trees' at Accettura in Basilicata (where a male and a female tree are joyfully united) still hark back to the ancient desire for divine blessing on all forms of life—not excluding snakes.

Indeed the festival of May at Cocullo in Abruzzi features five different kinds of snakes which are displayed by their handlers around the statue of St Dominic the Abbot, the acknowledged protector from snake bites.

Summer

In the summer, most cities and towns celebrate their 'national day', recalling the golden age when they were independent city-states, richer and more cultured (in their own eyes at least) than anywhere else. The festivities comprise a parade, a fair, competitive games, a mimic 'battle' and perhaps a joust, a tournament or a horse race.

In Florence, the highlight is the *Calcio*—a ball game in costume, which seems to be a mixture of rugby, American football, football and Greco-Roman wrestling.

In Pisa, the festival centres on the game of the bridge, contested by two squads who start at both ends and struggle for its possession as they did in the Middle Ages.

In Arezzo, like at Ascoli and Foligno, tournaments are held between teams from different parts of the town after a gorgeous parade in medieval costumes. Harking back to the clashes between Christians and Moors at the times of the Crusades, the target is often a figure representing a Moorish king.

Venice holds a spectacular historical regatta involving all sorts of rowing boats. Recently, too, regattas have been staged between the four 'marine republics': Genoa, Venice, Amalfi and Pisa.

But the most striking event of all is the famous *Palio*, held in Siena on 2 July and 16 August, when a parade of all the *contradas* in their traditional dress is followed by a brief but rumbustious horse race round the Campo, with the jockeys riding bareback and according to the medieval rules, no holds barred.

FOOD FESTIVALS

The Italian summer is also coloured by what are called *sagre*—less elaborate events centred on the local produce. These take place all over the country, and are far too numerous to list. Here are just a few:

- **Isernia (Molise)**: Sagra of the Onions—28–29 June
- **Viadana (Lombardy)**: *prosciutto*, melons and wine—28–29 June
- **Camastra (Sicily)**: bread in the shape of arms, legs, feet and hands—2 July
- **Ariccia (Lazio)**: *porchetta* (whole roasted pig) on the first Sunday in July
- **Peschici (Apulia)**: olive oil—20 July
- **Livorno (Tuscany)**: *cacciucco* fish soup—third Sunday in July
- **Teglia (Lombardy)**: *pizzocheri* pasta—last Sunday in July

Drinking coffee and people-watching
are popular pastimes in Italy.

- **Sissa (Emilia-Romagna)**: watermelons—last Sunday in July
- **Monteporzio Catone (Rome)**: apricots—last Sunday in July
- **Noto (Sicily)**: gelato ice creams—August
- **Montefiascone (Lazio)**: Est! Est!! Est!!! wine—August
- **Pievepelago (Romagna)**: blackberries and blueberries—August
- **Castel Gandolfo (Lazio)**: peaches—August
- **Saltara (Marche)**: *berlingozzo* sweetmeats—August
- **Felitto (Campania)**: *fusilli* pasta—August
- **Campofilone (Marche)**: *capellini* pasta—mid-August
- **Amatrice (Lazio)**: *amatriciana* pasta—third Sunday in August
- **Cortemilia (Piedmont)**: hazelnuts—last Sunday in August
- **San Daniele (Piedmont)**: *prosciutto* ham—last Sunday in August
- **Angri (Campania)**: tomatoes—September
- **Carmagnola (Piedmont)**: sweet peppers—September
- **Budoia (Friuli), Cera (Piedmont) and Santa Fiora on the Monte Amiata (Tuscany)** all hold a festival of mushrooms in September

Some places dramatise the presentation of their products. For instance at Porto San Giorgio in the Marche, calamaris are fried in a gigantic 15-feet-wide pan and offered free to the public, and the same sort of Gulliver-like pan is used to fry small fish at Camogli (Liguria) in May; while Lavagna (Liguria) produces a 19-feet-high cake in mid-August.

Visitors are welcome, indeed encouraged, to take part in these festivals. But it should be remembered that they are red-letter events on the local calendar, and would take place with just as much gusto even if there were not a tourist in sight.

POLITICAL FESTIVALS
In recent decades, the summer has been enlivened by festivals organised by the various political parties to

butter up the voters. Christian Democrats hold the *Festa dell'Amicizia*, Communists the *Festa dell'Unità*, Socialists the *Festa dell'Avanti*.

These events, which were important in the 1970s and 1980s, took place first all over the country, then in the regional centres, and reached their climax in national party rallies. They were an attempt to create a new kind of festival, with cultural shows, films and gastronomy harnessed for the benefit of politics.

It remains to be seen what the future holds in store for these festivals. In the last few years only about 40 per cent of those attending were party members.

AUTUMN

At the end of the summer cycle of festivities start the Italian football championships. Some people say that football represents the new festive cycle for Italians, made up of games, symbols and rituals which can be both serious and carnivalesque, yet at times dangerously violent. The playwright Eugene Ionesco believed that both theatre and football will have a great future, being 'useless necessities'. With football, Italians achieve local and national identity, as well as international acclaim. They can participate in World Cup matches while comfortably seated at home, or clustered in the stadiums.

And so they reach the end of the yearly cycle to *cenoni* (New Year's Eve dinner) or *veglioni* (dancing parties) where the year concludes in a burst of conspicuous, festive consumption.

SUPERSTITIONS

Like everywhere else, but perhaps more so in Italy, there are many folk beliefs that remain as a curious heritage from ancient times. Most Italians will claim that they are not superstitious, yet they will touch iron (as others touch wood) or a horn

There are ways to counteract bad omens. If you break a mirror, throw the pieces into a stream of running water; if you spill salt, throw it over your left shoulder three times; if you spill wine, cheers! It brings good luck. In southern Italy, you should touch the back of your ear with some of the spilt wine. Good luck is sure to follow.

of red coral, or even their testicles, to avoid bad luck or potential danger.

A black cat crossing your path is supposed to bring bad luck. But a ladybird signifies good luck, as does finding a four-leaved clover, or a seven-legged spider, a walnut with three rims instead of two or a coin on the ground.

It's bad luck to walk under a ladder or to sit 13 people at table (the apostles plus Jesus, with a traitor among them) and for this reason the number 13 is considered particularly bad. Often hotels do not have a room 13, or even a 13th floor.

As in ancient Rome, some days are reckoned to be unlucky, notably Friday 13 or Friday 17. An old proverb warns one not to marry, nor to leave on a journey or start an important project on a Tuesday or a Friday.

Among other common beliefs are the bad luck of putting a hat on a bed or of sleeping with one's feet pointing at the door (which is the way corpses are placed).

THE SEAMIER SIDE OF LIFE
The Drug Scene
Drugs are a serious problem among Italian youth, even if it has not reached the frightening level of most western

countries. Since 2003, law made illegal the possession of drugs as authorities stepped up in their campaign. In 2004, a total of 32,159 cases related to drug use, pushing and abuse were discussed in court and ended with a sentence of guilty. Addicts treated in public and private institutions were estimated to be almost 60,000 in 2003. The amount of drugs seized in 2003 was estimated at something around 19,000 kg (41,887.8 lbs).

The Mafia

The origins of the Mafia go back centuries to the time when Sicily was invaded by the Arabs and the Normans, and heavy-handed foreign domination provoked the inhabitants to set up a sort of underground government and legal system of their own.

It was only in the second half of the 19th century that Sicilian emigrants exported the concept of *cosa nostra* to the eastern United States (the 'Irish mafia' did the same) and there, unhappily, it became a much romanticised criminal organisation which in due course spread back to home base. Its Neapolitan counterpart is known as *Camorra*, the Calabrian one as *Ndrangheta* and the one in Apulia as *Sacra Corona Unita*.

The object of all these groups is the conquest of power and money by means of violence and corruption. In the 1980s, for instance, the homicides in mafia-controlled areas represented an average of 5.91 a year per 100,000 inhabitants in Naples, 6.80 in Palermo and 18.67 in Reggio Calabria. Compare these figures with Milan (where some mafiosi are present too) which has a yearly average of 1.37.

It's generally agreed that the Mafia is not a centralised organisation, but a territorial division of areas controlled by a few powerful families. Mafia crimes range from those directly related to its activities (such as drug trafficking and extortion) to those caused by inter-mafia wars and attacks against the forces of law and order—of which the assassination of General Dalla Chiesa in 1982 and Judges Falcone and Borsellino in the early 1990s are striking examples. Apart from drugs, it has made huge profits by controlling public works and recycling 'hot' money into legal activities both inside and outside Italy.

As recent confessions of ex-mafiosi have shown, the Mafia has had a long involvement with the ruling class and politicians in power. In return for favours, the Mafia has influenced the votes of the electorate, especially in Sicily. Recently, however, many important successes have been recorded in the struggle against the Mafia. Thanks to the evidence provided by ex-mafiosi in a series of show trials, a number of the top 'bosses' have been jailed. In 2004, 5,598 cases related to the Mafia were discussed in court and ended with a sentence of guilty.

Italy is one of the major fashion capitals of the world and the country has produced many renowned fashion designers.

Siena in Tuscany, Italy, is a UNESCO World Heritage Site and is one of the great examples of Italian romanesque architecture.

Italy offers a wide variety of fresh and exotic fruits and vegetables. A delivery truck on the streets of Cefalù, a major tourist destination located on the northern coast of Sicily.

Many Italians are passionate about football and are strong supporters of the national football team.

A lady enjoys an afternoon break as she reads the newspaper outside her shop.

SOCIALISING

CHAPTER 4

'We watched the ocean and the sky
together under the roof of blue Italian weather.'
—Percy Bysse Shelley

DRESS CODE

Like the French, Italian men and women have an inborn sense of style, and dress with elegance. Italian fashions are a by-word both for *haute couture* and casual sporting wear —their designer clothes are exported all over the world and bring a great deal of revenue to the national economy. Milan, Florence and Rome are the capitals of high fashion; Como is noted for silk, Florence for leather.

Nowadays, people dress very much as they like. In churches, of course, there is a tendency to show respect by wearing formal clothes, or at least a dress for women, a long-sleeved shirt for men and proper shoes. Women are required to cover their heads, and men to take off their hats.

When accepting an invitation, it is customary to wear a coat and tie for lunch, and a dark suit for dinner. In the country, one can be more informal.

Black tie affairs are rare and explicitly announced (renting a dinner jacket is not as easy as elsewhere) but on these occasions women come in long formal dresses, and give their best jewellery an airing. For cocktail parties women usually wear a short dress, men a coat and tie. In fact men can get away with a dark blue double-breasted blazer and charcoal grey trousers at all but the most formal functions. (Blue shirt in the morning, white in the evening, lighter trousers at the yacht club.)

By the same token, all that women need to fit into the social scene is a light suit for daytime, an elegant little cocktail dress and an evening gown. Teenagers, like their peers all over the world, wear jeans, shirts and sports shoes. Italian children are often said to be dressed like 'little people'—that is, like adults in miniature.

Jewellery

Italy is one of the great places for jewellery. Bulgari in Rome, Buccellati in Milan, UNO-AR in Arezzo and the many little goldsmiths on the Ponte Vecchio in Florence are renowned for their exquisitely-mounted jewels. (Gold is usually 18 carat, so check and calculate prices.)

Symbolism

Precious stones also have their symbolism. In Italy it is believed that:

- Crystal/silver/Moon = purity, transparency
- Pearl/copper/Venus = virginity, mysticism
- Diamond/gold/Sun = perfection, luminosity
- Emerald/iron/Mars = bravery
- Cornelian/tin/Jove = prosperity
- Turquoise/lead/Saturn = longevity

Elegant Italian women usually wear one ring, one bracelet, one pearl necklace or gold chain and one set of earrings—not to overload is the traditional imperative, both during the daytime and at formal gatherings. As its name suggests, the solitaire diamond needs no company to be fully appreciated.

Most men wear a gold chain round the neck with a cross or the image of their protector saint, and a casual watch. A ring and a gold bracelet around the right wrist are sometimes worn too, but avoided by those in the know as being a trifle tacky. Gold cuff-links and an elegant watch are sported in the evening and on special occasions. Young people tend to wear less precious jewellery (often eye-catching paste) in greater profusion.

Jewels are traditionally given as presents to celebrate important occasions: for births, gold and red coral against the

Many Italians still buy fresh fruit and vegetables from local greengrocer's and markets.

evil eye (ancient Romans did the same); at baptism, a gold chain; a gold watch on the 18th birthday; for engagements, a solitaire to the woman and a ring or cuff-links to the man; a gold wedding ring to the bride and groom; a brooch to the mother for her first baby; a diamond ring for wedding anniversaries (10th, 20th, 25th and so on).

RECEIVING HOSPITALITY

To be invited to an Italian home for dinner is a sign of strong friendship, for as a rule Italians do not entertain acquaintances in their own houses, but take them to a restaurant. So arrive on time, bringing flowers or a little gift. You'll be shown into a living room and introduced to the family and other guests.

Either an aperitif or a light white wine—often sparkling —will be served along with little titbits (what Americans call 'munchies') and these will give a clue as to what is in store: peanuts and potato crisps signal a normal meal, but if tasty

Four generations of Italians come together for dinner. The meal consists of spaghetti, cold meats and salad, ending with a home-made cake. Everything is washed down with Chianti red wine from the vineyard outside.

little hors d'oeuvres are produced you can look forward to a gastronomic feast.

After about half an hour of conversation you will be shown to the table. Do not take your drink into the dining room, for you'll find that glasses are on the table, carefully lined up in decreasing sizes. The left one is for water, and next to it come the wine glasses, white, red and, on the right, dessert.

The Dinner

Cutlery is laid out with the forks on the left, spoons and knives on the right, fruit and dessert silver behind the plates. (Use the outside cutlery for each successive course.) Napkins stay on the right, and if there is a small dish for bread it will be on the left. Make sure you don't use the one on your right, that's for your neighbour, and confusion will ensue.

The seating arrangements are the same as anywhere else. Your host will sit at the end of the table, with the oldest or most important woman on his right and the next in rank on his left; the hostess will be at the other end with the oldest

---

Social Etiquette

At Dinner

- The napkin should be put on your lap, not on the table.
- It is considered impolite to keep your hands on your lap in Anglo-Saxon fashion. Both forearms should rest on the table, but not the elbows.
- You use the fork with your left hand, the knife and spoon with your right, without any switching.
- When you've finished, leave your cutlery on the plate, spoons and forks pointing upwards, knives with the cutting edge on the inside.
- If you happen to spill some wine on the table cloth, don't be embarrassed; it's considered good luck. (But there's no harm in apologising, just the same.)

or most important man to her right, etc., and so on down the table, care being taken to separate couples (the rationale for that is because they stay together all the time). If your hostess is clever she'll try to sit people close together who have something to say to each other, or at least speak the same language.

You will be served from the left, and dishes or glasses will be removed from the right. Should space be limited, lean over to enable the waiter to do his job. (Don't help yourself from the dish when it comes on your right, it's being offered to your neighbour.)

When your turn comes the waiter will expect you to serve yourself. Better not take too much at first, because there'll be a second helping. But remember that if you say 'no thanks' you'll be taken at your word, and out of respect no one will insist on your having any more.

You're expected to drink what you like, but without making any appreciative noises. Italians, like the French, not only enjoy their food but like to talk about it while eating. This

- Chocolates, a bottle of wine or liqueur are appropriate presents when invited to dinner.
- Don't expect your host to open and offer the presents round—it would be rude to share them on the spot.

General
- Don't confuse gifts and tips. A gift is symbolic; a tip is a monetary payment for a service rendered by someone who may have been friendly but who is not a friend.
- Porters, waiters, taxi drivers and hotel commissaires expect a tip.

is an acceptable topic of conversation and gives you the opportunity to make a few polite remarks about the wine and the food you have been offered.

The lady of the house sits down first, starts eating first, and gets up first. So wait for her signal.

The dinner party ends with dessert and dessert wine. Smokers can then light up, unless it's made clear that the house is non-smoking. In that case, abstain or go outside. Though Italy produces some fine pipes as well as the famous Tuscan cigar, neither pipes nor cigars are widely smoked (and Havanas are virtually unobtainable). So if you wish to puff your cherished Partagas, ask permission from your hostess first. She is the one in charge of everyone's well-being and she will do her best to accommodate your desires too.

Taking Leave

It's up to you to leave at a reasonable hour. At the weekend you can stay until midnight, but on other nights it's advisable to leave earlier. Don't expect any hint from your hosts. No glasses of water will be passed round as a signal, like the custom was in the east.

If you leave early, justify your departure with the excuse of an early morning start or an international phone call that's expected. '*Grazie per la magnifica serata*' is a goodnight thank-you. Send a note the following day, with flowers if you feel inclined.

Tips for House Guests

It may happen that you're invited to stay by an Italian family, with what appears to be an open invitation to remain as long as you like. If so, don't take the generosity of your hosts too literally. Remember the old Italian saying: *L'ospite è come il pesce, dopo tre giorni puzza* (a guest is like a fish, after three days it stinks). No matter what you're told, make it clear from the beginning exactly when you'll leave.

Italians have an innate sense of space, so don't intrude on theirs. Stay in the room you've been given, and when you emerge make sure you don't disturb anyone. Find out who sits in this armchair or on that couch, and establish your own niche in the sitting room and your place at the dining table. Don't spread yourself and your things all over the house. If the bathroom is communal, keep your towels and beauty case in your room.

If you're encouraged to do so, by all means help yourself to whatever there is in the kitchen, but don't run your hostess out of pasta or wine, or polish off your host's favourite brandy. Tell them what you've taken, and mention that it was delicious.

There's no need to replace what you've used. Instead, it would be a nice gesture to buy them some unusual delicacy, and offer to cook a special meal from your own country. In that case, insist on doing all the shopping for it yourself. It's a present from you.

Clean up whatever you use. If you need to use the washing machine, ask for permission. On no account should you ask to use the car or the motor cycle.

Enquire if you may use your host's house as a contact address for post, telephone calls and especially visits. Ask if it's all right for someone to pick you up. Give the impression at least of being autonomous.

Every home has an established routine, so try not to disrupt it by adjusting your schedule accordingly. You will usually be given a set of keys. If not, ask for them on the basis that you don't want to disturb anyone with your coming and going.

Keep your host and hostess informed about your movements, because you are temporarily part of the family and they may get worried if you disappear for a few days. If you go off on a trip, send a postcard or phone them to say exactly when you expect to be back.

Offer to help around the house, but don't insist too much. Your hosts want you to be a guest, not a waiter or a kitchen maid.

At the end of your visit, write a thank-you note, leave a gift and if there are servants, leave a tip for them in an envelope.

All of which is simply common sense and normal etiquette. But as you will have noted, there are certain aspects of being

A bunch of flowers is always a safe bet when invited to an Italian home. Florist shops are stocked with fresh flowers every day from the countryside and they do good business supplying bouquets and wreaths.

a guest in Italy that may differ from what you are used to, and it is just as well to know what these are.

Gifts and Tips

It's not a bad idea to bring a few typical little items from your home country to offer as presents to the families you meet. A gift for the children will win the hearts of both the kids and the parents. No need to bring anything too big: it's the thought that counts.

Flowers or a plant will always be welcome. But avoid chrysanthemums, which are associated with funerals. For some reason the colour purple has implications of bad luck (though not always: it was worn by prostitutes in the Renaissance). Roses are usually offered in bunches of a dozen, or uneven numbers—seven or five.

If you give someone a handkerchief, ask for a small coin in return, otherwise it will bring tears. (The coin symbolically repays the gift and eliminates the bad omen.)

It will be considered specially thoughtful if the gift takes your friend's hobby into account. If he collects stamps, bring the latest set from your country. If she is fond of embroidery, some needlework from home will be greatly appreciated.

More than the actual value of the gift, your friends will be touched by the fact that you took time and trouble to find something appropriate—a painted glass, a Balinese fan, a bit of Tiffany deco silver, a book or a view of their town printed in your home town, even postcards sent to your country from Italy.

VISITING CARDS

Three kinds of calling cards are used in Italy. The business card is a public one, being used for business relationships, personal promotion and in the professional sphere of the person's life. It refers to what you do in life. On this you can add your business email address and your business mobile phone number.

The social card carries all the social status, titles and honours. For example, if you are a Count by nobility, and Commendatore for your civic achievements under Republic, plus you have a Ph.D., you may write Conte Commendator Dottor on your social card. You can also add your personal email address and your personal mobile phone number.

A third card is used for personal or even intimate correspondence. The recipient is supposed to know only your name. You may add by hand whatever else you want, including street address or cyber address, you may add a few words or a few lines on this card. While you are at it, use a nice old-fashioned fountain pen and write in real ink—black or dark blue, and weight well each word.

Italians normally use larger visiting cards than people in the USA, Britain or the Pacific region. If you want to follow the Italian convention, you should have one card with just your name embossed, preferably in small capital letters, to accompany personal messages or gifts when you don't want to parade your professional or social titles.

Similarly with letterheads: business stationery and faxes will indicate all professional titles, but for private correspondence the stationery (which may be used by house guests) will have the address on the back of the envelope without any phone number and a letterhead giving the address plus phone number if desired. The colour of the stationery is preferably pale grey, white, beige or light blue.

CAFÉ/BAR

The bar, sometimes called a *caffè*, is Italy's answer to the British pub, the French café or the German *Bierstube*. It is a place where people gather to have an espresso, a soft drink or something more potent.

Italians take three or four espressos every day. Sometimes more, a habit which is sometimes jokingly said to be the reason for their lively character and even livelier temper. If you don't appreciate the single-sip espresso, ask for a *caffè americano* in a large cup. Cappuccino, also known as *cappuccio*, is an espresso plus milk foamed up. Italians drink it for breakfast with a *brioscia* or croissant, but never after a meal. If you really want one, they'll usually produce it with a shrug of the shoulder. On the other hand, coca-cola drunk with meals will set their teeth on edge. Should you not wish for wine, mineral water will not raise any hackles.

Latte macchiato is warm milk with an espresso poured on it. Decaffeinated coffee is often called by its most famous brand name, 'Hag'. *Caffè corretto* has been 'corrected' with a tot of brandy or *grappa*.

Most bars provide a selection of pastries and small salty titbits, tiny pizzas, ham rolls (which tend to be dry) or

Bars and cafés are social centres. Italians love to gather at the café with the whole family to spend a convivial hour or two drinking, chatting and playing cards.

tramezzini (delicious sandwiches). Washed down with a glass of wine, such fare helps to beat the high cost of living. The regional varieties are worth exploring.

Literary circles used to meet at cafés, sporting groups still do, and every town has its landmark—such as Doney in Rome, Quadri and Florian in Venice and Rivoire in Florence —where local socialites gather to 'coffeehouse' leisurely.

CONVERSATION

When you talk about Italy, remember that Italians take more pride in their region than in the country itself. They are usually most willing to give directions to a stranger, especially if you look smiling and helpless. A few complimentary words about the local cathedral or monument, or even the vineyards, will win them over.

When enquiring about the negative aspects of national life (such as bureaucracy, politics or the high cost of living) give them a chance to set the record straight. Your object is to elicit information, not to preach. So don't lay down the law or voice your disdain. It's far better to adopt a slanting approach, such as 'I read that such and such...'

In Italy, there is always time for a chat with friends.

In Italy time is not money yet. You'll find that most people are delighted to spend the time of day in pleasant conversation. Do not thank them 'for having given you their time.' Thank them rather for the pleasure they gave you with it.

Loud as Italians may seem to you, believe it or not they often complain that tourists shout louder! So speak normally. They'll like you for it.

Introductions

In polite usage, it is customary to introduce the lesser person to the more important one, the man to the woman, the younger to the older. For example: '*Le presento il Dottor Chang*'. If no one is around to do this, say: '*Buongiorno, sono Bessie Brown*'.

Should you not catch the name of the person you've been introduced to, say, '*Mi scusi, non ho capito il nome*' (excuse me, I didn't get your name). This won't be considered a *faux pas* because people love to have their names remembered. (Napoleon capitalised on this all his life.)

If you happen to be seated when someone is introduced to you, you'll stand up if you're a man but not if you're a woman, unless you're meeting someone of great importance or prestige. Don't be limp-wristed or give a bone-breaking squeeze. Women or elderly persons offer their hand, or give a very small bow of the head. A word or two about the people who are being introduced is quite in order, and may be an opening for conversation. But always be brief.

Conversation Starters

You can ask, '*Di che cosa si occupa?*' (What do you do in life?) or '*Da dove viene?*' (Where do you come from?). But on no account should you ask people how much money they make. If your curiosity is aroused, enquire indirectly. For example, when speaking to a physician, ask '*Quanto guadagna un dottore?*' or '*Quante tasse paga un dottore?*' in Italy. Or start by saying how much a doctor earns in your own country, and ask your Italian acquaintance to offer a comparison.

It is permissible to mention politics—always an engrossing subject among Italians—but don't be provocative about the political set-up. Let them tell you how awful it is. And don't air your views about religion too jokingly, because you may be offending other people's susceptibilities.

SMOKING

It is forbidden to smoke anywhere in public. Some restaurants have areas for smokers, but usually outside. Smokers in forbidden areas are supposed to be fined so if you do smoke, be sure to know where to do it or ask. Most Italians, including the majority of smokers (65 per cent) agreed to this new law banning smoking in public.

MAKING A PHONE CALL

Mobile phones are now ubiquitous in Italy. They are also available for rent in certain *Negozi di telefonia* (telephone shops) where you can also recharge your mobile phone if it runs on a card. Buying or renting a mobile phone in Italy may be convenient compared to using your portable mobile phone from home to make local calls in Italy. Your call from Rome to Naples may go through, but via New York or Singapore! In any case, before you leave get the correct information about

In Italy, there is still a wide variety of authentic food to choose from.

who pays, and how much when you receive a call in Italy from your country, and when you make one. Access codes and numbers are also important, and you should obtain these before you leave home.

It is much more expensive to put IDD calls through from your hotel than from a public telephone. SIP offices are to be found in all major towns. Go to the desk and ask for a *cabina* (booth). For most calls you can use a *scheda telefonica* (phone card) worth 5 or 10 euros which can be bought at tobacco shops or newsstands. If the *scheda* runs out while you're talking, insert another one.

If you use someone's phone, it should only be to make a local or emergency call. Otherwise make *una R* (a collect call).

Italians say '*pronto*', not 'hello'. So if you want to say, 'Hello, I'm Nancy Kwann, I'm looking for Doctor Rossi,' you should say in Italian, '*Pronto. Sono Nancy Kwann. Vorei parlare con il Dottor Rossi.*'

SIESTA

The afternoon nap, or *pisolino*, dates from the ancient Roman custom of taking off the *sexta* (sixth) hour of the day, namely noon, because dangerous ghosts were supposed to lurk around outside. Today it is still an attractive feature of Italian life for those who can break the day and digest their lunch. But the *orario continuato* is gaining ground, so check what's going on between 1:00 pm and 4:00 pm.

SOCIAL CUSTOMS

Social customs in Italy refer to the rites of passage marking the progression of the individual through the age classes which are part of the society. These are:

- **Baptism:** over 95 per cent of Italians are baptised.
- **First Communion:** Catholic introduction to the mystery of being in touch with Christ.
- **Coming of age at 18 with a Debutante's Ball:** collective, upper class similar to the popular one in Milan or individual. At the age of 18, an Italian is directly responsible towards society and the law.

Italy is famous for its beautiful architecture, as seen here at the Piazza della Repubblica in Florence.

- **Engagement/Wedding:** 83 per cent are religious ceremonies, the remainder being civil ceremonies. Getting married in Italy is becoming fashionable. Many agencies in North America and Asia offer package deals including ceremonies in churches or city halls, flowers, bouquets, refreshments, rental of clothes, accommodation for the wedding guests and the honeymoon. Marry now, pay later (even in instalments).

- **Funeral:** the public mourning of family, friends and the community. Civil memory and religious prayers take place so that the deceased person goes into the other life. Prayers and masses help the spirit of the deceased, according to Catholic religion.

SETTLING IN

CHAPTER 5

'Thou Paradise of Exiles, Italy!'
—Percy Bysse Shelley

FORMALITIES
Residence Requirements
Citizens of the EU and US-passport holders do not require a visa or residence permit to visit Italy, and a *permesso di soggiorno* is no longer necessary if you stay longer than three months.

Nationals of other countries should consult their local Italian consulate concerning the documentation they need. As the regulations tend to change in line with EU directives, it is as well to check up on the prevailing requirements.

Civic Status
Until recently, a foreigner remained a *straniero* and a breed apart, even after spending a lifetime in Italy. Unlike in the UK, the USA, Australia and some other countries, it was difficult if not impossible for a foreigner to become an Italian national except by marriage.

This meant that you were excluded from the polls and had no right to vote in a national election or referendum. (Italians may have envied this dispensation.) However, in line with EU regulations, these stringent rules are being progressively relaxed. Election propaganda is already finding its way into foreign residents' post boxes. And in due course all EU citizens should enjoy the same rights as Italians. Reciprocal arrangements already exist with other EU countries, such that EU nationals who are entitled to free medical care or education for their children in their home country will usually find they can get the same privileges in Italy. US citizens should consult their embassy for up-to-date information.

Red Tape

Italian bureaucracy is a law unto itself, and Byzantine in complexity. Things that are taken for granted elsewhere often involve endless paperwork and a lot of legwork too. But things are easing up.

For visitors, however, there will be little need to get caught up with officialdom. If you acquire a property, you will have to get a *carta fiscale*, but it is not necessary to apply for permanent residence. Just register with the Commune.

But to buy a new car in Italy you must still produce a certificate of residence from your Commune or at least sign an affidavit that you are a resident there.

FINDING A HOME

If you are sent to Italy on business, your firm will dictate where you will live, and help you to settle in. You may be offered the option between a flat in town or a suburban villa, but whatever your preference is, you can expect to walk into

Documents Required

- A valid passport
- A current visa covering all your planned stay in Italy
- A driver's licence valid in Italy
- Health documents. If you need to buy medicine in Italy, you need a prescription from an Italian doctor or a doctor practising in Italy. Your Embassy or Consulate usually has lists of doctors practising in your area speaking your language. If you bring prescription medicine, bring also your doctor's prescription.
- If you plan to study in Italy, bring an official transcript from your school or university. It will speed up application and enrolment.

it fully found. And should you be required to find your own accommodation, professional advice will be provided.

Renting A Place

Renting a house or a flat is relatively simple. The agent will advise you about the rights and obligations of a tenant. For a short lease, or a holiday letting, it is usually unnecessary to make a notarised contract. Yet at least a letter of intent signed by you and the landlord may be a good idea. Clarify if utilities are included or not in the price you pay for the rent. Usually a deposit is required, and the landlord will give it back at the end of the rental, less breakages and damages.

Choice of Location

It's a different matter if you decide to retire to Italy for good, or acquire a holiday home. You will be following a long tradition. Foreigners have been living in Italy for centuries, and at the present moment over a million are residing more or less permanently in various parts of the country. Numerous foreigners, especially Germans, have acquired holiday homes in the Gargano promontory.

Built in 1250, the oldest fortified mill in the Marche still functioned until a few years ago. Subsequently an author's hideout, it was recently bought and redecorated by a well-known London designer.

They are chiefly to be found in or around Rome, Florence and Venice; around the Italian lakes north of Milan; on the Sorrento peninsula, Capri and Ischia; in southern Tuscany, Umbria and now the Marche. There are scattered groups of expatriates along the Ligurian riviera from San Remo to La Spezia, at Palermo and Taormina in Sicily, around Trieste and at the Costa Smeralda in Sardinia. Northern Latium and Abruzzi are becoming increasingly popular too.

Very little of Italy remains undiscovered. New *autostradas* and airports have made most of the peninsula easily accessible. Your choice will therefore depend on your own personal considerations.

You will have to decide what you are looking for. Weather will be an important consideration. The famous Italian sun is more elusive than you imagine, and parts of the country, especially the north and the Apennines, can be perishingly cold and damp between November and April, with heavy frost, fog and violent storms. Even in Rome the temperature in January is sometimes lower than in London.

The climate is much warmer along the coast and in the south (though in winter you will need layers of clothes indoors and in the evenings). By the same token it can become exceedingly hot in summer.

But remember that the whole coastline is seething with holiday makers in July and August, and often as dead as a door nail during the winter months.

For carefree outdoor living with reasonable amenities to hand, you will probably do best to select the central part of the country between Florence and Rome if you are thinking of settling in Italy. By and large that means Tuscany and Umbria, which are the favourite haunts of foreigners (and more geared to their needs) as well as being the nation's cultural heartland. The Marche is also a good bet for many people.

Finding A Property

Maybe you have friends who will help to smoothen the way. Otherwise, select a region you feel you may like, and give it a thorough consideration.

You may fancy a Florentine *palazzo* (or at least an apartment in one). But first rent a flat to see what living in Florence, Rome or Venice really means. Once confined to a busy city with its own distinctive ways, you may find the culture shock overpowering, unless you have intellectual interests that enable you to participate in the social life.

Many people have found it better to live out in the country, and come into town whenever they feel inclined.

The British, for instance, have always made a point of living 35 minutes' drive from the centre of Florence. A century ago, they dwelt at Bellesguardo or Settignano; now they and other foreigners have farmhouses in Chianti, which is 35 minutes away by car or bus.

So how do you find your dream house in Chianti, or elsewhere?

Drive through Tuscany and Umbria to get the feel of the land. When you come across a corner that appeals to you, book into a hotel, or better still, rent a furnished farmhouse —there are plenty of them available by the week on a self-service basis—and case the joint.

Forty years ago there were 60,000 empty farmhouses for sale in Tuscany. You simply went into the nearest bar and asked what was available; a helpful character (usually the local *mediatore,* or land agent) would hop into your car and show you a dozen properties. If you were interested in buying one, he would find the owner and conduct negotiations; sometimes a *compromesso*, or preliminary contract, would be written out and signed over a glass of wine.

Nowadays things are different. Very few empty farmhouses remain on the market, and real estate agents handle those that are. You may still find what you want on your own, but you will need professional help to negotiate the purchase.

Having viewed several properties, how do you make your choice? See (metaphorically) whether your name is written on the door. As a prominent Lloyd's underwriter used to say when appraising a risk, you'll feel it in your water.

Bargains are few and far in between in Italy today. There are still a few areas in the central regions where you can still pick up properties at relatively low prices. These are:

the Garfagnana, Monte Amiata, the Adriatic foothills of the Marche and the Casentino in Tuscany.

Points To Watch

When assessing a rural property, the three most critical points to look for are: water, electricity and approach to the road.

Water

Some farmhouses have main supplies but some still don't. They rely on a spring or an artesian well. Make sure that the spring is on the property, or that the well doesn't dry up in summer.

Electricity

Most farms are hooked up to the grid. If not, it can be an expensive and sometimes lengthy business to install electricity, and this should be reflected in the price of the property.

Means of Approach

That delectable little shepherd's house at the top of a hill may only be reached by a rocky path going through other people's land, which is impassable in winter. A reasonable approach road is essential—you have to use it all the time—and will be expensive to make, especially if rights are involved.

Other Points to Check

- The roof, in many ways, is the heart of the building. But paradoxically, a roof in poor shape is not necessarily a deterrent, because you will perhaps be wise (and the authorities will probably insist) to rebuild it from scratch according to the antiseismic regulations. It's really a question of cost.
- The walls are more important. Make sure there are no bulges at the corners or ominous cracks.
- Wooden beams should be checked too. If rotten, they could bring down part of the roof or the floor. However, dry rot can be treated.

- Rights of way and other existing lines on the property should be clarified and written into the contract.

Such matters are best handled by an architect, a *geometra* or a surveyor. You would do well to take professional advice before signing a *compromesso*, which is the preliminary contract. At this point you will be expected to make a down payment, the exact amount to be fixed by mutual agreement with the seller.

The *compromesso* endows you with certain rights, but with obligations too. If you fail to complete the deal, you are liable to forfeit your deposit, or at least part of it. By the same token, if the seller revokes, he will have to return the deposit plus an equivalent amount, unless special circumstances prevail. Since this can lead to wrangling, it is wise to have the *compromesso* drafted by the notary who will stipulate the final contract, or at least done by the *geometra*.

The choice of notary lies with the purchaser, who must pay the costs of the contract, as well as the balance of the purchase price, upon signing the final contract. The seller is responsible for INVIM (capital gains tax) but only that prior to 1992.

Another hazard is the fact that the land authorities will subsequently—often months later—make their own assessment of the value of the property, based upon a complex set of equations. If, as often happens, this is more than the contract price, both buyer and seller will be faced with an additional tax. Beware: the property remains as security if the seller reneges on this. The notary, who is a government official, will advise you about such matters.

Moreover, if the property is registered as *rurale*, i.e. agricultural, it is important to ensure that none of the adjoining land is owned by *coltivatori diretti*, that is, farmers who have pre-emption rights, which they are entitled to exercise within a year. (It has happened that an unsuspecting purchaser has been deprived of his property months after buying it. So insist that such neighbours sign a discharge.)

Fixing Your Property

You'll need help. First of all, a permit to restore the property must be obtained from the local commune. This means employing a *geometra*. The *geometra* will draw up detailed plans, and will submit them to the competent authorities, including in most cases the antiseismic officials. In accordance with your instructions, he will redesign the house for you, even make arrangements for a swimming pool if you wish, and find contractors to do the work. In fact, he'll act as architect.

Remember, however, that although trained as an architect, the *geometra* is basically a land surveyor and all too prone to adopt the plodding, cliché-ridden style of modern Italian houses. In other words, he is unlikely to be very imaginative. There are exceptions!

By contrast, an architect may turn out to be far too imaginative, treating your house as an opportunity to try out some bombazine experiments. Turning an Umbrian farmhouse into a Californian ranch is the very last thing you want.

In short, *geometra* = conventional; architect = showiness. (There are notable exceptions, of course, but by and large that's the gist of it.) The choice is yours. If you have acquired an ancient and perhaps historic building, you may have to consult experts from the Belle Arti. Their advice will keep you on the straight and narrow, but could be a bit restricting.

Once the designs have been finalised, you must wait (sometimes months) for the local commission to deliberate and give their approval. There will also be a tax to be paid. Finally the builders will get to work, along with carpenters, plumbers, electricians, bulldozers, uncle Tom Cobley and all.

This is an exciting time, something of the salt of life which you should not miss. Many people simply go off after leaving instructions with the contractor—and return the following Easter (usually with a clutch of guests) naively expecting to find the job completed.

Of course it never is. And they've lost all the fun of watching their new home taking shape. Nothing is more thrilling than to settle down in the neighbourhood and follow the day-to-day progress.

Useful Documents
- Project signed by a technician
- Authorisation to begin work by the Commune of Residence
- At the end of the work, signed documents from the firm doing the work, the plumber and the electrician

---

Mind you, it won't be roses all the way. There will be plenty of frustrations—workmen who casually vanish, fluctuant problems that won't, disasters which crop up in accordance with what is known as sod's law, bureaucratic hassles that make the head spin like a dervish—but at least you'll have the satisfaction of being involved in the game, and be on the spot to put right any gaffes which have been innocently overlooked.

While the work is going on, you'll have plenty of time to comb the countryside for furniture and equipment. From the flea market in Florence or the antique market in Arezzo (first Sunday of every month) you may pick up some attractive odds and ends. Or try some second-hand shop such as the chain of Mercantino. This is a local franchise with outlets independently operated. It is present in many cities and sells on commission almost anything you may require for your new home.

By roaming around you will discover villages, even towns, hardly touched by tourism, and have a chance to get to know the people in your own commune.

For them you will always remain *stranieri*—the Americans who are restoring the old tower on the crag, the English who have taken over the mill, or the Germans who are fixing up so-and-so's dilapidated farmhouse. But you will soon be drawn into the everyday life of the place. And the more remote it is, the more co-operative friendliness you will encounter.

Instead of trying to rush matters, you will learn to take it easy—*a l'italiano*.

WHAT TO BRING FROM HOME

It may be a good idea to bring the following to assist you in your stay in Italy.

- A heavy line of credit
- A good dictionary
- An official transcript and an official copy of your education certificates. Also copies of documents witnessing in detail your school career ie. courses taken, grades, etc.)
- If you have any redundant furniture which you wish to bring with you, fill a container and ship it over. The shippers will deal with the formalities. You are allowed to bring into Italy 'first installation' furniture and standard household goods. However, as Italy manufactures almost everything you will most likely require, it is usually cheaper and more practical to buy what you need on the spot. Top-class Italian antiques are probably the only exception to this rule for while run-of-the-mill items proliferate, the really good items, including paintings, often cost less in places such as London or Paris than in Italy itself. The finely crafted reproduction furniture that Italy produces might also be worth considering.

Pasticceria
MAIOLI

Pastry shops can be found throughout Italy.

THE EDUCATION SYSTEM

It is obligatory for Italian children to go to school between the ages of six and 18, but once their basic education is completed, about 20 per cent of them try to find a job and do not pursue any further studies.

Most of the schools are public, administered by the central government (though elementary schools usually come under the local commune) but there are also a few which are run by private or Catholic organisations. All of them, however, take the same set of state-controlled exams.

Pre-Primary and Primary Education

At the age of three, children can go to a public or private kindergarten, known as the *asilo* or *scuola materna*, and 90 per cent of the toddlers do.

The *scuola elementare* (or primary school) begins at the age of six and continues until the child is 11. Children are taught Italian, mathematics, history and science, often with the help of images and music. But as the lessons only last four hours a day, such things as sport and religious instruction take place outside the normal curriculum.

Intermediate School

The *scuola media*, or intermediate school, lasts for three years. Classes are co-educational, with an average number of 25 students. Boys and girls study Italian literature, history, geography, mathematics and also a foreign language. Subjects such as basic technology, art, music and physical instruction are usually regarded as extra-curricular activities.

High School

To qualify for the *media superiore*, or high school, an exam known as the *diploma di licenza media* must be passed and at this point specialisation begins. Students choose between four disciplines: classical, technical, professional or artistic.

- Classical studies are further divided into four branches: *Classico*, which stands for humanistic training (Latin, Greek, history and philosophy); *scientifico* (much the same, but with maths and sciences); *linguistico* (emphasis on modern languages); and *magistrale* (for those who intend to teach in elementary schools).

- Technical training is a preparation for practical jobs. The *istituti tecnici* are industrially-oriented and turn out accountants, surveyors, agriculturists, business executives, tour operators, air traffic controllers and so forth.
- Professional discipline concentrates on practical careers in electronics, chemistry, computers, catering, advertising and the applied arts.
- Artistic stream involves a four-year course of studio art or architecture.

Finding a School

- Check the White Pages and the Yellow Pages in your area.
- For public schools, each province has a *Provveditorato agli Studi* so it is best to talk to the *Preside* (Principal) of the school you are interested in.
- In addition, you can check with your Consulate for information on foreign schools in your area.
- Also check at the Commune with the *Assessore all'Istruzione* (local government for education and schooling).
- Public schools are usually much less expensive than the private ones.

University

At the age of 18 or 19, students take the *maturità* (roughly the equivalent of the French *baccalauréat*) or a technical diploma. Anyone who passes these exams is entitled to go on to university or polytechnic. Currently Italy has over a million undergraduates—almost two per cent of the population, and twice as many as in Britain. Since these academies don't offer residential accommodation, most of the students live at home and attend the local university.

Except at top-notch places such as the Bocconi in Milan, the LUISS in Rome and some medical schools, tuition is free and there is no limit to enrolment. Consequently the lecture halls are so crowded that sometimes it's almost impossible to squeeze in. A minimum of four years is necessary to obtain a degree, and students can choose when they want to take the exam; if they botch it the first time they can have another go.

There are two state universities for foreigners: the Universita per Stranieri at Siena and a similar one at Perugia. These institutions are reserved for non-Italian citizens who are regularly enrolled in a university abroad, or whose academic standing entitles them to have access to them.

Foreign Schools in Italy

There are a large number of foreign schools, both private and public, which are run either by Italian or by foreign administrators and teachers. These establishments range from small kindergartens to post-graduate branches of famous American universities. If you are coming to live in Italy, or intend to make a prolonged stay, we suggest that the best plan would be to contact your embassy in Rome or the local consulate, which will be able to provide guidance.

Day Care Centres

Day care centres in Italy are called *Asili Nido* or *Scuole Materna* and are both public and private. Many will take children either five or six days of the week. The public ones have quotas and strict regulations since they are supported by the state.

Normally, you will be expected to drop your child off at 8:00 am or 8:30 am and collect them again at either 4:00 pm, 5:00 pm or 6:00 pm. The private day care centres are more flexible and, depending on which one you choose, you will be able to pick up and drop off your child whenever you need to. In both public and private day care centres, children will eat lunch at the centre, which is prepared under sanitary control and planned by a dietician. The cost of a typical private nursery is 100 euros for application and entrance fees and 150-200 euros per month, thereafter. This includes meals.

MANAGING YOUR HOME

Domestic help is often available, but becoming increasingly difficult to come by. It used to be possible to engage the services of a married couple. The woman would clean the house, cook a bit and do the laundry; the man would look after the property, tending the vines and olives, gardening, and maybe driving the car.

Nowadays such couples are hard to find and expensive to maintain. The going rate is something like 15,000 euros a year, including social security etc., and they will expect the free use of a house with all expenses paid.

Sometimes arrangements can be made with old age pensioners who are no longer subject to social security. But more usually people make do with a woman who comes in for a few hours each week, the going rate being around 9–10 euros an hour. A jobbing gardener who is employed for, say, half a day twice a week will expect to be paid about the same amount. But check around to see what the local rates are, and specify from the start exactly what you want done.

BANKS

If you are a resident, you are entitled to have a domestic account like any Italian citizen. If not, you can open a non-resident account, which can only be replenished by transfers from abroad. Should you wish, the bank will settle your electricity and telephone bills when they become due, and also make any regular payments that are necessary. The arrival of the euro has signalled many changes. For up-to-date information, consult your bank manager.

TAXES

Fiscally you are behoven to the commune in which you reside. In turn, the commune is controlled by the regional authorities, and may be bound by different regulations from those obtaining in other parts of the country. Residents (and house owners) pay a tax on the rental value of their property, as well as certain local and wealth taxes. Most people use the services of a *commercialista* (accountant) to handle their tax matters. You would be well advised to do the same.

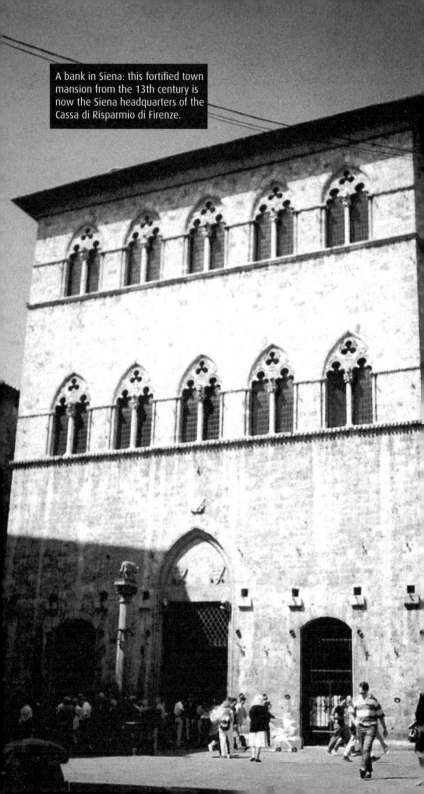

A bank in Siena: this fortified town mansion from the 13th century is now the Siena headquarters of the Cassa di Risparmio di Firenze.

Useful Information

- Before you leave, check with your bank if it has a correspondent bank in the area of Italy where you are going to live. It may be possible to have matters prepared from your homeplace and ready for you to double-check and sign when you arrive.

- Check the entrance regulations. If you bring money or financial instruments with you, for a high amount, you may have to declare them on your arrival.

- See the Direttore of the local branch of your selected bank in Italy.

- Enquire about the services you need. Costs may vary from bank to bank.

- Almost all banks issue a BANCOMAT card that you can use instead of cash to pay for many goods and services. In addition, you can use it to obtain cash and other services such as recharging your portable phone directly from the cash points that are prevalent throughout the country

SHOPPING

Supermarkets abound in every town, and hypermarkets —whole shopping complexes—are to be found at strategic locations. In most places, too, there are now speciality food shops (known as *gastronomia*) where you can fill yourself to the brim with costly groceries. However, the village shop still thrives and remains the focal point of social life. It is where people exchange gossip while collecting their daily provision of meat, vegetables, cheese and bread.

Italians like to buy frequently and in small quantities so that the ingredients are fresh. No bulk buying for them. They want to be sure of getting the freshest and most genuine local produce, without any nonsense such as injecting meat with hormones to improve the taste, or vegetables and fruit with colouring matter so that they look good on the supermarket shelves.

And then on an appointed day, practically every village has its open-air market, which is the highlight of the week. It is

Italian jewellery is famous
throughout the world.

In addition to selling you fresh fruits and vegetables, your greengrocer is quite prepared to burst into operatic aria.

the occasion when people from the surrounding countryside get together to transact their affairs or just pass the time of day, and a good opportunity to corner your elusive plumber or have a word with the mayor.

WHAT THE MOTORIST NEEDS TO KNOW
Traffic Rules
At intersections where there are no traffic lights, the vehicle on the right has priority. In fact the rule of the right applies almost everywhere (in the cities many drivers hardly give a glance to the left) except at certain roundabouts and on main roads which display the priority sign. This is a yellow and white lozenge on the right-hand side of the road. If it has a black line across it, you don't have priority. Many intersections and roundabouts are marked with arrows. These should be followed carefully to avoid getting into the wrong lane by mistake.

Traffic Lights
Traffic lights work the same as elsewhere, but the amber stays on for several seconds. This leads to drivers running

through the red, or hooting angrily if you stop as soon as the amber light appears.

On some arterial roads you'll come across a big red light with smaller green arrows below. When a green arrow lights up in the direction you want to go, you should drive on even though the red light seems to indicate the contrary.

Speed Limit

In Italy, the speed limits are 130 kph on the *autostradas*, 110 kph on four-lane highways, 90 kph on normal roads and 50 kph in urban areas.

Safety Tips

- Fasten your seatbelt.
- Don't drink and drive.
- Breathalysers (nicknamed *palloncini*) are used throughout Italy.
- Watch the signs. The large square sign marked *'Controllo elettronico della velocità'* means that there may be an electronic machine ahead checking your speed and taking a picture of your car. If you speed, they will send you a stiff bill at the home address of the person or company who owns the car.

Italians used to take little notice of these restrictions, but nowadays they do. Police and radar traps abound; if you are driving way above the limit, you may get landed with a 'super-fine' amounting to as much as 500 euros. A nasty habit is to photograph the car without your knowing—until you receive a massive fine by post a month later. The speed ticket will also follow you all the way to your country of residence, due to recent reciprocal agreements between countries.

Foreign-registered Cars

You may be safe driving a foreign-registered car, but don't bank on this. And don't be lulled into security by the sight of a few cars speeding by. A new form of one-upmanship is to disregard the fines ('I'm so rich I don't care').

Remember too that it's an offence not to carry your driving licence and passport with you, as well as the car

Driving in Italy is unlike anything you have experienced before. Manoeuvring between parked cars along narrow cobbled streets will put your driving skills to the test.

documents. Failure to do this could cause embarrassment if you're stopped by the police.

Often you'll suddenly be flagged down by a posse of *carabinieri* with automatic guns at the ready. This is because of terrorist and criminal activities. It's an unnerving experience, but fortunately they deal gently with foreigners.

Italian Driving

Italians are reputed to be cut-and-thrust drivers, but on the whole they stick pretty close to the rules. Some have an annoying habit of riding your rear bumper on twisty roads. Just signal them to overtake as soon as you can.

Incidentally, it is mandatory in Italy to signal any change of direction—such as overtaking, turning or stopping—with your signal lights. And if you do have to stop on the road, place your red triangle sign a few yards behind the car.

Communicating with Other Drivers

Inter-driver communications are important. Make eye contact with a smile, and the angriest, most aggressive face at the wheel will suddenly relent and let you through. After all, you're the guest. If he doesn't, for heaven's sake don't make a rude gesture. That can lead to real trouble. After all, it's his country.

POSTAL SERVICES

The postal system, it must be admitted, used to suffer from a vein of dispraise. Ordinary post was expensive and often deplorably slow, sometimes taking a fortnight to reach its destination in a nearby province. But postal efficiency has noticeably improved, and if a letter is sent *espresso,* or if you pay a small supplement, it will normally arrive within a couple of days. Choose *posta prioritaria* (priority post), registered or not, and your letter, envelope or package will be delivered worldwide within days. Standard boxes of differing sizes that can be sent worldwide are also available at post offices. In addition, the post office handles administrative matters such as the payment of pensions. It will make remittances for you, and also accepts *Poste Restante* mail. To collect letters you have to produce a proof of your identity.

Except in the main cities, post offices do not offer telephone facilities.

TELECOMMUNICATIONS

The telephone system is efficient, but expensive. You can phone IDD worldwide from almost anywhere. Mobile phones have become fashionable, as well as facsimile machines. The Internet has caught on, and you can send e-mails from specialised shops in most towns, resorts and villages.

HOUSES OF WORSHIP

The Italian Constitution guarantees total freedom of worship. However, the state religion is Catholicism and Italian culture has Catholicism at its root. The Catholic Church is the centre of the Italian social structure and a centre of power as well. So it is no surprise that every town or small village has at least one Catholic church. Nearly all Italians have been baptised in church, but only about 40 per cent are practising Christians.

Other religions are also practised in Italy. Houses of worship are found in all regional capitals and in the main cities. Check the *Yellow Pages* for addresses.

FOOD AND ENTERTAINING

CHAPTER 6

'Drama, drama, drama! The Italian meal is like an opera.'
—Waverley Root

THE FOOD OF ITALY HAS SPREAD ROUND THE WORLD. What, after all, could be better on a cold winter's day than a piping hot bowl of minestrone or *spaghetti alla bolognese* fragrant with Parmesan cheese?

But the popularity of pasta and pizzas has led to the belief that Italians live mainly on macaroni and veal, tomatoes and olive oil, washed down by Chianti from a straw-covered *fiasco*.

Nor has the home-grown hotel industry done much to dispel this illusion. Restaurants on the tourist circuit tend to dish up such fare, often because it is economical to make. Known as 'international', this type of cooking bears the same relation to real Italian food as 'pidgin-Italian' does to the language of Dante.

Italians themselves think in terms of regional cuisine— Venetian, Florentine, Milanese, Neapolitan and so forth— rather in the same way as the Chinese differentiate between Cantonese and Sichuan, Hakka and Hokkien.

Through the centuries every region, every city even, has developed its own culinary talents. Each is subtly different, and if the sum total constitutes the signature of Italy, it is because they are linked by common eating habits and a common larder.

Individuality dominates. Someone once said that whereas the French are amateurs who cook like professionals, the Italians are professionals who cook like amateurs. "Order a *béarnaise* sauce in 200 different French restaurants and you will get the same sauce 200 times," comments Enrico Gallozzi, the Italian gastronome. "Ask for bolognese sauce in 200 different Italian restaurants and you will get 200 different versions of *ragù.*"

This diversity of cuisine is part of Italy's culture, not to mention its charm. It must be sampled region by region. So once again let's start off with the north.

Did you know...?

Data from the CIA (Confederated Italian Agriculture producers) indicates that in 2004, each Italian consumed 123 kg of wheat products, including 28 kg of pasta, per person. Also, 195 kg of vegetables, 130 kg of fruits, as well as 50 litres of wine and 14 kg of eggs. The Mediterranean diet, based on fresh produce from the local market and from the current season, is still alive and well in Italy, despite increasing globalisation.

PIEDMONTESE FOOD

Piedmont borders with France, and the influence of Savoie is evident in its food. Up in the mountains, few households had ovens until quite recently, and cooking was done in a frying pan or by boiling.

Hence the *bagnacauda,* literally the 'hot bath'. A sauce is made of olive oil, butter, garlic, chopped anchovies and thinly sliced white truffles. This is served in little bowls on individual heaters with a selection of raw vegetables which you dunk into the mixture.

Truffles, Rice and Meat

White truffles go into many Piedmontese dishes, including the *fonduta*, a variation of the Swiss *fondue*. And since Piedmont produces much of the country's rice, you'll find plenty of risottos.

Agnolotti (ring-shaped envelopes stuffed with minced veal, ham and spices) are the favourite type of pasta. But *tagliatelle* cooked in chicken broth and served with chicken livers comes

You can buy all manner of cheese from small local shops. They also stock cured meats such as hams and salami, and will often make up sandwiches for customers.

a close second. Much *polenta* is eaten, as well as *semolina gnocchi*, which is said to have originated here.

Bollito misto—boiled beef, chicken, veal and ham served with cabbage or onions with a green sauce and a dab of jelly —is a popular dish. Others are *brasato al Barolo* and tripe stewed in white wine.

Vegetable Dishes

Clever things are done with vegetables. *Panizza* (a speciality of Vercelli) is a mixture of white beans, tomatoes, onions, bacon and rice. Peppers are stuffed with tomatoes, anchovies, garlic, butter and then baked; mushroom heads, stuffed with parsley, onions, anchovies, egg and bread crumbs, are simmered in olive oil. Truffles are stewed in Asti Spumante, or cooked with Fontina cheese. Onions are made into a sweet by stuffing them with bread soaked in milk, macaroons, scrambled egg and raisins.

Indeed Piedmont is famous for its sweets—the streets of Turin are lined with confectioners where you can pile on the calories. Turin is also the home of the humble *grissini*, or bread sticks, which stand like logos on the tables of Italian restaurants all over the world.

PIEDMONTESE WINES

The vineyards around Alba produce Piedmont's great Barolos and Barbarescos from Nebbiola grapes.

Barolo is one of the most famous of all Italian wines. Grown in a carefully defined territory just south of the Tanaro River, it has a bouquet of violets and a smooth velvety flavour with a slightly resinous aftertaste—known as *goudron* or tar.

Barbaresco, which comes from the steep slopes surrounding the ancient town of that name, is also a 'big' wine—a younger sibling of Barolo if you like—and it matures more quickly.

Wine from north of the Tanaro is simply called Nebbiolo and has the violet fragrance which is characteristic of that grape. These vintages are lighter and can be drunk young.

Piedmont wines are predominantly red. But among the whites, Asti Spumante has become famous ever since Carlo Gancia, who learned how to make champagne at Rheims, got to work on Moscato grapes.

Nowadays Asti Spumante is as common as vermouth, another Piedmontese speciality which originated,

Italian wines are famous all over the world. But, on a hot summer day, there's nothing more thirst-quenching than a swig of cool water from the village fountain.

commercially at least, in 1786 by Benedetto Carpano at his wine shop near the Turin Stock Exchange. It seems that the dealers' cries of *'punt e mes'* (a pint and a half) went into the language, like Carpano's own name, to describe a special type of bitter vermouth which is made of white wine infused with herbs, spices, roots and a good many other ingredients.

In those days, the vermouth producers were small family affairs. Now they are mammoth distilleries whose secret formulas are jealously guarded. Some 50 million bottles of Italian vermouth are consumed every year, and the classic cocktail, dry martini, is named after the most celebrated producer: Martini & Rossi.

LOMBARD FOOD

Lombardy is known for agriculture as well as industry. Employing the most modern methods of food production, it reaps more wheat and corn per acre than any other region in Italy, and grows more fodder. Vast quantities of sheep and pigs are raised, not to mention some two million heads of cattle each year, which yield a sea of milk and a mountain of butter.

Lombardy cooks almost entirely with butter and one of its chief products is cheese—Gorgonzola, Bel Paese, Mascarpone, Taleggio, Robiola and more Parmesan than Parma itself. In Milan, you'll find the world's greatest cheese shop, La Casa del Formaggio, which opened a century ago and offers hundreds of different types, along with side-products such as cheesecakes.

Milan has always adopted an extravagant attitude towards food (at one time it was decreed that only those who produced their own bread or wine would be eligible for public office), and even today the Milanese believe in doing themselves proud.

Lombard Specialities

Yet, unlike the other regions, Lombardy does not have any typical dishes of its own, except *costoletta alla Milanese,* or breaded veal cutlets, from which the Austrians got their

Wiener schnitzel. (The only difference is that they fry it in fat, whereas the Milanese use butter.) This is a very ancient dish and it featured on the menu of a banquet held in Milan as early as in 1134. It was the Austrian General von Radetz who imported it to Vienna many centuries later. Another is *ossobuco*, which everyone seems to cook in a different way, though they all agree that it should be served with rice rather than mashed potatoes or pasta.

In Milan, pasta plays only a minor role. A meal usually starts off with a lavish display of *antipasti*, followed by a risotto, gnocchi or stuffed pancakes known as *crespelle*. This is so often followed by *busecca* (tripe) that the Milanese are sometimes called *busecconi* (tripe-eaters).

Beef pot-roasted whole in red wine is known as *manzo alla lombarda*. By contrast *cazzoeula* is a pork stew with a difference. Ribs, trotters, crackling, even a pig's ear go into the pot along with sausages, cabbage, celery, onions and tomatoes. Served with mounds of steaming *polenta*, this rib-sticking fare is calculated to keep out the cold on a freezing night.

> The most frequent fare is *scaloppine*, which are presented in all sorts of ways but preferably breaded. Alternatively there may be *lesso misto*, a local variation of *bollito misto* served with *salsa verde*.

LOMBARD WINE

Lombardy has three wine-producing areas: Oltrepò Pavese, an extension of the rolling hills of Piedmont; the Valtellina, along the valley of the river Adda which flows into Lake Como; and around Brescia on the western banks of Lake Garda and the Mantuan hills.

Of these the purest Lombard is the Valtellina valley. Its distinctive wine is Sassella, which has a dry, lively flavour of roses (Virgil mentions it in the *Georgics*).

Other top-of-the-line reds are Grumello and the lighter Inferno.

Just as the Oltrepò wines are almost Piedmontese, so the Lake Garda vineyards are on the edge of the Veneto and produce wines similar to Bardolino and Soave though not so well-known, including one called Lugano which sounds slightly displaced. However Lombardy does make one famous drink—Campari, produced in Milan since 1867.

THE FOOD OF EMILIA-ROMAGNA

Emilia-Romagna is a region of sparsely populated hills and bustling plains where every inch of land is put to use. This is pig country, wheat country, fruit and vegetable country, even fish country (if such a neologism is permissible) and these abundant resources have made it the nation's gastronomic centre.

Parma is famous for its ham and its cheese; Modena for *zampone* (stuffed pigs' trotters), cherries, peaches and macaroons; Bologna for pasta and *mortadella* (of which the American copy known as baloney is genuinely bogus, as Edith Sitwell would have said); the province of Ravenna for seafood. The local chefs have done the rest, turning some of their restaurants into places of pilgrimage for gourmets.

Parma Specialities

As a matter of fact there is a hint of baloney about Parma's claims, for Parmesan cheese actually originated in Reggio, which still makes most of it. But since Reggio once formed part of the Duchy of Parma, we'll not argue the point.

Nor is Parma ham produced in the city itself; it comes from the hills in the south of the province where conditions are ideal for raising hogs and curing hams. Langhirano, which is the centre of the industry, literally lives and breathes ham during the drying season when gammons are suspended from every ceiling of every room in the town.

Sadly, Parma violets have all but vanished, but the perfume industry they inspired still thrives along with a great variety of sweetmeats and particularly good cooking. Try *tagliatelle* with Parma ham or *melanzane alla parmigiana*—aubergines done with smoked ham, onions and tomatoes. And a simple grilled cutlet topped with crisply fried parsley. Delicious!

Modena and Bologna Specialities

In Modena and Bologna the cuisine is heavier, because they use more butter and lard than olive oil. Furthermore, pork

dominates the menu, in every shape and form but especially as plump spicy sausages.

Modena was probably making *zampone* in the days of the Romans, and exactly what goes into the pigs' feet is a closely guarded secret. Nutmeg, cinnamon, cloves, garlic and pork mince are certainly ingredients.

Bologna's *mortadella* descends, it is said, from the Roman *murtata* and is made of highly spiced pork mince packed into the skin of a whole suckling pig. But Bologna is above all the home of the northern type of pasta which is made with eggs, as opposed to the coarser southern version which isn't. The city's great trinity are *tagliatelle*, reputed to have been created in honour of Lucrezia Borgia's golden hair, *tortellini*, considered to be as shapely as Venus's belly button, and lasagne, which the Romans called *laganum*.

Of course Bologna has many other types of pasta: a culinary expert once listed over 600 variations. And although pasta and sausages loom large on the menu, they by no means overshadow the main dishes. You should try *costolette alla Bolognese*, which is breaded veal (sometimes turkey) covered by a slice of ham. It becomes *scaloppine alla Bolognese* when slivers of meat are cooked with alternate layers of smoked ham and potatoes.

Involtini are rolls of veal with a stuffing of spiced chopped meat served with *ragù; umido incassato* is a luscious veal casserole made with chicken giblets, sweetbreads, beaten egg yolks, truffles and mushrooms in béchamel sauce. Even suckling pig is simmered in milk flavoured by truffles, and when chicken appears on the bill of fare it is likely to be covered in mutton paste, mushrooms and béchamel on a bed of ham, onion and spinach purée. This pièce de resistance is called *canestrelli*.

Desserts and Seafood

Desserts are just as rich, and you'll find high calorie repasts at Ferrara, along with eels from the lagoon of Comacchio and sturgeon from the Po. It is a relief for the digestive juices to reach the coast, where fish is king.

Nobody cooks seafood better than the Italians, and no sea is a finer habitat for fish than the northern Adriatic which (unlike the rest of the Mediterranean) has tides. This means tidal pools and seaweed which help the propagation of shellfish and crustaceans. For seafood lovers, the combination is supreme.

THE WINES OF EMILIA-ROMAGNA

Lambrusco, the famous wine from Modena which bursts into a pinkish foam when poured into your glass, raises the eyebrows of connoisseurs who are horrified at the idea of a sweet fizzy red. Though it can hardly be classed as a quality sparkler, genuine Lambrusco goes well with the rich local food and is quite different from the 'Lambrusco-cola' that enjoys such success in the United States. The best is Sorbara, a ruby red wine with a pronounced flavour of violets.

More distinguished are the San Giovese reds cultivated on the south side of the *autostrada* leading from Bologna to Rimini. These are dry, with a taut aftertaste.

Even better is the golden-yellow wine produced from the Albana vines south of Forli, which are not grown anywhere else in Italy. Legend has it that the Empress Galla Placida was so delighted with the bouquet that she exclaimed "*Voglio berti in oro*" (I want to drink you in gold). She said it in Latin, of course but the name Bertinoro has stuck.

VENETIAN FOOD

Venice, like Milan, prefers rice to pasta. *Risi e bisi*, a simple partnership of rice and fresh peas, is one of the Veneto's most enduring specialities.

Venice also prefers seafood to meat. The variety of its rice-cum-fish offerings is astonishing. You can have rice with eel, with sole, with fresh anchovies, with lobsters, scampi, mussels and even with oysters. A delicious combination, if you are not put off by the colour and like a strong fishy taste, is black rice made with the ink taken from squid.

Risottos are also made with tripe, chicken livers, frogs' legs and quail. Even the humble *risotto di secoli*, made of butcher's left-overs, is an appetising dish.

Meat dishes

While not shunning meat, Venice likes to disguise it. Stews are preferred to grills, and if *polpette di carne* are tastier than ordinary meatballs, it is because they are blended with egg in a seasoning of candied lemon, pine nuts, grapes and brandy.

Being fond of poultry, Venetians do splendid things with chicken and turkey. For example, a capon is sewn into a pig's bladder with pieces of beef and guinea fowl before being boiled. To make *anitra alla salsa piccante*, a wild duck is marinated overnight in vinegar, thyme and tarragon. Then it is buttered, covered with thin slices of bacon and put into the oven for 15 minutes. After that the bird is cut into pieces which are simmered in a sauce made of wine, anchovy fillets, onions and capers. It comes almost as a surprise to find that *fegato alla Veneziana* is simply liver and onions—a dish the Venetians claim to have invented.

Venetian Seafood

What Venetians love best, of course, is fish. A meal usually starts with a seafood *antipasto*, which may include oysters topped with local caviar, followed by the local variation of bouillabaisse known as *brodetto*.

The fish for the main course is simply cooked but accompanied by an elaborate sauce, the recipes for which would fill a book (even mackerel fillets come with a sauce made of butter, flour, egg yolks, lemon juice, vinegar, white wine, onion and spinach). Moreover Venetians have a partiality for cold fish. You will be offered fillets of sole served on ice with pine nuts and grapes, mullet with parsley and orange slices, and little breaded fish of every species perfumed by a variety of herbs. You may also be given cold lobster in its shell on a bed of lettuce, topped by a sauce of mayonnaise, brandy and cream.

Regional Food

What the city eats goes for the region too: gastronomically Venice predominates from Verona to Trieste. Even Padua with its famous old restaurants and cafés (many political plots were hatched at the Padrocchi) owes much of its gourmet reputation to Venetian influence, though the Bolognese touch emerges when it comes to pork.

Verona has a fondness for *gnocchi* and fresh fish from Lake Garda. Vicenza, whose gothic buildings and frescoed facades have been described as 'Venice on land', has a dish—chicken cooked in a clay pot—which harks back to Longobardi days. Turkey and pigeon, as well as snails, are local specialities.

Further afield, Belluno goes in for simple mountain fare, with an emphasis on beans and polenta. Treviso offers freshwater crayfish which you hold in your fingers and suck. Eels can make up a whole meal, starting with eel risotto and going on to roast eel, fried eel, boiled eel, whatever you fancy. Jugged hare is also a speciality.

Friuli, a relatively poor agricultural area, lives mainly on poultry and vegetables. But at Trieste, the Venetian influence reappears. Like Venice, Trieste favours seafood and rice. Its cuisine has an Austrian flavour, with goulash and strudels to the fore. Two specialities are *bruscandoli* (asparagus with an egg sauce) and *liptauer,* a do-it-yourself platter of cheeses and herbs, which you mash together to suit your taste. When it

Waiters can help you decipher the menu if you are unsure what to order.

comes to pastry, Trieste has as many types of cakes, tarts and fritters as Venice and Vienna combined. A cookery book lists no less than 285 varieties.

WINES OF THE VENETO

The Veneto produces over 850 million litres of wine a year, most of which is agreeable plonk. Only about 91 million litres are DOC, mainly made in the vicinity of Lake Garda. The province of Verona alone turns out the region's most reputed red vintages, Bardolino and Valpolicella, as well as the best white, Soave.

DOC

DOC = Denominazione di Origine Controllata

DOGC = Denominazione di Origine Controllata e Garantita

The Bardolino vineyards lie between the Brenner *autostrada* and the lake, just to the northwest of Verona. Clear ruby in colour, Bardolino is usually described as 'charming', meaning that it is light and refreshing.

On the other side of the Adige River are the vineyards which produce Valpolicella. This is a good deal heavier, a dark velvety red with a slightly bitter aftertaste of almonds.

Left of the Serenissima Autostrada heading towards Venice is the Soave district. Soave means 'suave' in Italian, which is a fair enough description of the light straw-coloured wines that are in fact named after the town of Soave in the middle of the vineyards. Some 40 million litres of Soave are made every year, but as a great deal more than this is actually sold, it is as well to check that your bottle bears the DOC label.

The Breganze area behind Vicenza and the Euganean hills north of Padua produce a cluster of above-average vintages. Further east around Treviso and Conegliano there is an explosion of good table wines, reds and whites as well as the sparklers bottled under the collective name of Prosecco.

The Tocais made around Asolo and Maser are not heavy and sweet like the great Hungarian Tokays, but light pale yellow wines which go well with seafood. Some of the Friuli wines deserve to be better known, and the same holds true for those of Trieste.

LIGURIAN FOOD

Liguria uses everything that grows under its benevolent sun. But the cuisine was shaped by Genoa's maritime vocation. It was tailored for sailors who yearned for fresh food.

Hence the prevalence of aromatic herbs—especially basil, from which pesto is made—and ravioli, which can be stuffed with left-overs. The Genovese make a cult of pesto, and stuff everything possible with all manner of ingredients. (You will find ravioli filled with seafood or even fruit). They go in for thick soups such as *sbirra*, made of tripe, and *burrida,* the local version of fish stew. Because of the high quality of Ligurian olive oil, most meat dishes tend to be fried.

Above all, the Genovese make great use of the fish that swarm around the coastline. Fish is put in salads, soups, stews and the sauces for pasta. Indeed their great dish is *cappon magro*, an elaborate seafood and vegetable salad built on a base of sea biscuits and shaped as a decorative pyramid.

LIGURIAN WINES

Liguria is said to have 65 varieties of wine, but only two are well-known. Dolceacqua comes from the hills behind San Remo, and white Sciacchetra from the Cinque Terre near La Spezia.

TUSCAN FOOD

Tuscany is renowned for the simplicity of its cuisine, which relies on the blending of flavours and contrasting textures. Tuscans are fervent meat-eaters and their great speciality is *bistecca alla fiorentina*—a luscious T-bone steak from the Val di Chiana beef grilled on a wood fire with a touch of oil and pepper.

In theory, any dish styled *alla fiorentina* is likely to have spinach in it. Don't be fooled, the label often means

In Tuscany, grilled rabbit is sold along with chicken and chips from a specially-equipped van.

something quite different. For instance, *fegatelli alla fiorentina* consists of chopped pig's liver with fennel. Risotto is cooked in meat sauce with chicken giblets; *zuppa di fagioli* (white beans) is made with onions, garlic and tomato sauce—a favourite Tuscan combination.

In umido means stewed in red wine, onions, garlic and tomatoes, which is how lamb and chicken are often cooked; when mushrooms are included it's called *alla cacciatora*. *Arista* is loin of pork roasted on a spit; *pollo alla diavola* is devilled chicken.

Game is a great feature and so are songbirds. The repertoire includes wild boar, pheasant, jugged hare (*salmi di lepre*), stuffed partridge (*starna*), thrushes on a spit (*tordi*), larks and woodcock (*beccaccia*).

Pasta specialities are *pappardelle alla lepre*—a sort of lasagne made of hare stew—and cannelloni stuffed with a mixture of meat, chicken livers, truffles and cheese.

Pisa boasts of its frog soup, Livorno of its seafood—which is nearly always cooked in oil with tomatoes (try the red mullet, the mussels and the fish soup called *cacciucco*).

WINES OF TUSCANY

Tuscany means Chianti. The region produces other wines, but this is what counts. The name comes from *Clanti*, which is what the Etruscans called the hills between Florence and Siena where the most celebrated vineyards are located. The wines from this area are known as Chianti Classico; their imprimatur is the old emblem of the medieval Lega del Chianti—a black cockerel in a red and gold circle.

Steeped in history, these Gallo Nero vintages are made mainly with Sangioveto grapes, blended with Canaiolo (the grape of the Etruscans, it is said), white Malvasia and Trebbiano, in accordance with a formula laid down by Baron Bettino Ricasoli a century and a half ago.

There are some 800 producers in the DOC zone, whose vintages are strictly controlled and propagated by the Chianti Classico Consorzio. Some major growers also experiment with slightly different mixes which they market under their own name without putting a black cockerel label on the bottle.

All are full-bodied wines with a smooth yet aggressive tannin tang, and most of them have been given an extra fillip by the addition of specially prepared over-ripe grapes at the moment of fermentation, a process which dates back to Roman times and is known as *governo*. Only when the wine has been matured for at least four years in the cask can it be labelled *Riserva*.

Some acceptable white wine is made too, but never called Chianti. A speciality is the tawny dessert wine known as *Vin Santo*, of which Queen Victoria was so fond.

Apart from the high octane Classicos you will find a number of other DOC Chiantis—such as *Putto*, *Ruffina*, *Colli Fiorentini*, *Colli Senesi*, *Colli Aretini*,, *Colli Pisani* and *Montalbano* —which make equally good drinking but are not quite so well-known.

Nor should you miss two wines which are among the glories of Tuscany: Brunello di Montalcino, and Vino Nobile di Montepulciano. Both are noble reds from just south of

Siena. Among the whites, try Vernaccia di San Gimignano, and Montecarlo from the hills east of Lucca.

Mind you, there are two types of Chianti. That which comes in raffia-covered *fiaschi* or half-gallon bottles is a lively, all-purpose *vin du pays*. But what upholds the reputation of Tuscany are the 100 million litres of DOC wine that are made every year in well-defined areas—of which the most important is Chianti Classico.

There are over 250 major producers of Chianti Classico, and some of the top wines are marketed worldwide.

The Super-Tuscans

Lately, some grand cru wines, the so-called Super-Tuscans, have become fashionable among the wine connoisseurs all over the world. The most acclaimed is Sassicaia, produced in Bolgheri near Leghorn by Marquis Incisa della Rocchetta. Other famous Super-Tuscans from the same area are Ornellaia and Masseto. Tignanello is produced by the Marquis Antinori not far from Florence. Be prepared to pay something around US$100 for each of these rare, fashionable, magnificent wines.

UMBRIAN FOOD

Umbria's cuisine is honest and natural, like that of Tuscany, but a bit less refined. Food to fill body and soul, but not to catch the imagination. Meat and pasta feature prominently because this is beef and wheat-growing country. Umbria also produces black truffles (Spoleto and Norcia used to be the truffle centres of Italy) and a wide variety of mushrooms.

Umbria's speciality is *porchetta*—suckling pig generously seasoned with pepper and herbs and usually spit-roasted. Another is *agnello all'arrabiata*, known as 'angry lamb' because it is cooked on a raging high flame.

Palombacce, or white doves, may not be to your taste. But there is plenty of game, and besides trout from the mountain streams, the *lasca*, or roach, from Lake Trasimene is considered a great delicacy.

Local gourmets like to emphasise the 'sober genuineness' of Umbrian food, which comes from excellent raw materials and simple cooking.

UMBRIAN WINES

The only well-known Umbrian vintage is Orvieto, a pale yellow dry wine with a delicate perfume and a sharp aftertaste. Like elsewhere in central Italy, it is made of Trebbiano and Malvasia grapes.

Umbrians will tell you that the reds from the Trasimene hills resemble Chianti. Tuscans disagree.

FOOD OF THE MARCHE

In the Marche you will find two distinct types of food, according to whether you are in the hills or on the coast.

Inland Cuisine

'Rough and savoury' is how gourmets describe the inland cuisine, which is typical of central Italy except that lamb and pork are the favourite meats and stuffed olives abound, especially around Ascoli Piceno.

Macerata claims to make the best *porchetta* and to have invented the regional speciality, *vincisgrassi* (named, euphonically, after the Austrian Prince Windischgratz) which is an extremely rich sort of lasagne. Also, being pig country, the smoked ham from this province is reckoned to be even softer and tastier than Parma's *prosciutto crudo*.

Coastal Cuisine

Cross an invisible line about 20 km (12.4 miles) from the coast and you are in a different world, dominated by delicious seafood of which the symbol is *brodetto*. Fish soup is to be found everywhere along the Italian seaboard from Trieste to San Remo, but the *brodetto* of the Marche is a feast for the Gods. In Porto Recanati, which is considered to make the best, it is flavoured with saffron and stuffed so full of fish —especially rock-fish—that you can hardly find the liquid.

WINES OF THE MARCHE

Although the Marche is not noted for wine, few wine-drinkers have not heard of Verdicchio, 6.5 million litres which are sold around Italy and exported in amphora-shaped bottles. A bright straw yellow with a clean dry taste, it is made around Iesi from Verdicchio grapes plus a touch of Trebbiano or Malvasia, and accounts for half the Marche's DOC production.

The rest is Rosso Piceno and Rosso Conero, which are full-bodied, ruby-coloured wines with a distinct nutty taste. Both have recently appeared on the international scene, including supermarkets. At an international blind tasting in New York in 2000, a Castelli di Iesi vintage was awarded top honours.

THE FOOD OF ABRUZZI AND MOLISE

This is mountain country where cows and sheep graze on the high plateaux and every little town has its own specialities. The local cooks are expert with lamb and make delicious warming soups, liberally lacing the food with cheese, chilli and sharp mountain herbs.

Their skills are brought together in the *panarda*, a traditional banquet of at least 30 courses which, when you think you have reached the end of the meal, it starts all over again.

WINES OF ABRUZZI AND MOLISE

This was once an important wine area and still produces some reasonable vintages—such as Montepulciano d'Abruzzo, white Peligno, Rocca del Falco and a rosé called Cerasuola —though they are not widely known today.

APULIAN CUISINE

Apulia has a very old civilisation and its historical background has created a variety of cuisines. On the coast, you'll find seafood of all sorts, often presented with some sophisticated refinements (the mussels are sterilised with ultra-violet rays.) But inland the cooking is peasant-like in spirit.

A lot of offal is eaten, and along with lambs' innards come the ubiquitous *orecchiette*—'little ears' made of kneaded flour, which trap the *ragù*—as well as delicious vegetables and salads. There are many varieties of pasta, but the *ragù* is almost invariably made by adding vegetables to a meat sauce base. This is tastily seasoned by using onions instead of garlic, except in the case of *spaghetti alla zappatora* (ditchdigger's spaghetti) which reeks of chopped garlic and red pimentos.

In Italy, a variety of hams and cheeses can be bought in local shops depending on your tastes.

Seafood

If Apulians eat little meat apart from offal and sausages, it is because they eat so much fish, which is both cheaper and more suited to the climate. Try the fish soup of Gallipoli, made today as the ancient Greeks made it, or Taranto's version which includes oysters. In Brindisi, fresh anchovies are baked in the oven with bread crumbs, and black mussels with potatoes. Eels are often cooked simply by the heat of the sun.

APULIAN WINES

Apulia produces over 200 million gallons of wine a year, much of which is used to cut northern wines and serve as the basis for vermouth. Strong heady stuff, it is mostly drunk directly from the cask. But choice grapes are processed separately and bottled under names such as Torre Sveva and Castel del Monte in memory of the Emperor Frederick II.

***

The Ones to Look Out For

San Sevaro is a label to look for (the reds are made from a blend of Montepulciano d'Abruzzo and San Giovese grapes; the whites from Trebbiano and white Bombino.) These wines, like the straw-coloured Locorotondo from the Trulli area, have such a high alcoholic content that they can last for years. There are dessert wines that reach 17 degrees, the best known being Moscato di Trani—made of the same grapes that go into Asti Spumante.

***

THE FOOD OF BASILICATA

Basilicata has always been poor country, and has a tradition of making do with very little. What goes into its dishes is local and undoctored, but highly seasoned with chillies, red pimentos and ginger—you'll find them even with fried eggs.

WINES OF BASILICATA

If Basilicata likes its food hot and husky, there is not much to wash it down. The region's wines can be dismissed with one name—Aglianico del Vulture, which is heady, pomegranate-coloured, and not bad at all. For an aperitif, try the slightly sparkling white Aspringo.

CALABRIAN CUISINE

Calabria's cooking is based on pasta, vegetables—and pig, which is turned into a huge variety of sausages and cured meats. These three staples are usually put together in the same pot, and as a result the most common meal comprises a thick soup, followed by cheese or fruit. Calabrians will tell you that soup does seven things: 'It appeases your hunger, slakes your thirst, fills your stomach, cleans your teeth, makes you sleep, helps you digest, and puts colour in your cheeks.'

However a culinary revolution is now taking place and seafood of all kinds—ranging from swordfish and tuna to *baccala* and pickled octopus—appears on the menu alongside old recipes which have been updated to suit modern tastes.

You'll find delicious specialities such as thinly-sliced swordfish with a lemon and oil dressing, stuffed aubergines, olive and garlic dip and spaghetti with snails. Also that most typical of Calabrian dishes, *morseddu*—which is a hash of pig's innards seasoned with tomato sauce and spices, spread on a crusty base that can be held in the hand like a pizza.

CALABRIAN WINES

Calabria does not produce much wine, and what there is can blow your head off. The only DOC vintage is Ciro, a dry red resembling Marsala in taste which is grown near Catanzaro.

Savuto used to be exported to the United States for homesick Calabrians; it should be drunk with discretion unless you enjoy nursing a hangover. At Squillace you will find Greco di Gerace, which requires two vines to produce a litre of wine, but of a delicate quality and anything up to 19 degrees in alcoholic content. The snag is, it costs a bomb.

In Italy, cafés and bars are seen as places to socialise and meet with friends.

SICILIAN CUISINE

Sicily produces vast quantities of grain, wine, vegetables and olive oil, as well as most of the country's citrus fruits—you can smell the scent of lemons and oranges wherever you go. But the old Arab domination of the island still influences the food. Sweetmeats like those displayed in the streets of Tangiers or Tunis form the basis of Sicilian cuisine. Even its famous ice creams come from the sherbets that kept Saracens cool in the desert.

Both *cannoli* (cylinders of sweet pastry filled with honey and almond paste) and *cassata* (creamy sponge cake combined with vanilla ice cream and spotted with bits of candied fruit) were inherited from the Saracens; just as marzipan, which appears in so many Sicilian confections, comes from the Arabic *martaban*.

Contrasting Flavours

Sicilian cooking is full of strange combinations of flavours and contrasts—for example *caponata*, made with lobster, octopus, aubergines, hard-boiled eggs and covered in chocolate. Most dishes tend to be a crazy but elegant medley of colours and shapes.

Meat may not feature prominently on the menu, but small game—being at the end of everyone's gun—does, and you are likely to be given wild rabbit with aubergine in a honey and vinegar sauce.

Pasta asciutta comes in many forms but a favourite is macaroni and cheese, baked in the oven with the ubiquitous aubergine.

Seafood abounds, and so does the *rosticceria*—a feature of Sicilian life which offers stand-up snacks at practically all hours of the day and night, usually based on some complicated manipulation of bread (such as buns filled with cheese, salami and meat sauce; or béchamel sauce with a purée of chicken and peas).

SICILIAN WINES

Marsala (named after the Arab port of Marsa Ali) is Sicily's best-known wine. In the hope of competing with port and

Madeira, John Woodhouse began developing the west Sicilian vineyards in 1773 and soon Marsala became a favourite wine in England.

It is made by adding wine alcohol to the local white wine and then pouring in boiled must, which is what gives Marsala its tawny colour. The result is a very sweet wine, but the sugar content is burned up in the cask. So the older the Marsala, the drier it will be.

Every province of Sicily has its own wines, but most of them are found only on the spot. Exceptions are the red and white Corvo (meaning 'crow') di Salaparuta from Palermo, which find their way into ministerial banquets as well as Alitalia flights.

NEAPOLITAN FOOD

Campania means Neapolitan cooking, and that of course means tomatoes. Pasta, eaten in Naples since Roman times, tends to mean macaroni or pizza.

In the past long *ziti*, that is hollow tubes of pasta, were hung to dry out on the sails of windmills (along with the washing). They were then broken into shorter pieces which were eaten *al dente*, crispier than anywhere else, with fresh tomatoes that were hardly cooked either.

It was in the streets of Naples that pizza was invented —perhaps the earliest fast-food of all. The original pizza had a simple topping of tomato and garlic. It was called *marinara,* which had nothing to do with seafood.

All the usual Mediterranean fish are available, usually fried, and *zuppa alla marinara* is made of whatever fish happens to be around. But be cautious about ordering *zuppa napoletana*—the chief ingredients are chopped pig's heart and lungs (plus oesophagus and windpipe) along with tomatoes and onions.

Capozzella ('little head') is roasted lamb's head. Typically, its brains are sauteed with bread crumbs and capers. Pork chops are referred to as *alla napoletana* when cooked with peppers and mushrooms. Be careful not to get confused with *insalata alla napoletana,* which does not contain lettuce, but cauliflower with anchovy fillets.

WINES OF CAMPANIA

Pliny, Horace and Martial waxed lyrical about Falerno—which is nowadays a not very notable dry white wine produced north of Naples, along with large quantities of fruity but often tart red.

Nor is the famous Lacrima Christi from the slopes of Vesuvius remarkable for anything but its pretty name and the fact that it has plenty of imitators.

What your Neapolitan will choose is Gragnano, a full-bodied red wine from the Sorrento peninsula. This has a pleasant nutty flavour, but is on the sweet side (and has a slightly off-putting purplish foam).

A better bet is white Capri, which goes wonderfully well with shellfish.

THE CUISINE OF LAZIO

Roman cooking is Etruscan cooking, say the gastronomes. It is like the Tuscan cuisine, but more exuberant in character. The city's zest and earthiness is expressed in its food. Full of strong flavours, this tends to be greasy and heavy.

Not surprisingly *porchetta*—suckling pig roasted whole on a spit—is symbolic of Rome. So are dishes made from whatever's left over in the slaughterhouse (including hearts, guts, tails and testicles.)

When in Rome...

- *Abbacchio*—baby lamb which has never tasted grass, spit roasted or cooked in the oven with rosemary
- *Saltimbocca*—thin slices of veal skewered to slices of ham and braised in Marsala
- *Coda alla Vaccinara*—oxtail chunks simmered in wine with celery and tomato sauce
- *Stufatino alla romana*—a rib-sticking beef stew
- *Pollo alla Diavola*—grilled chicken (lashings of pepper make it as hot as the devil)

Continued on the next page...

... from the previous page

- *Suppli al telefono*—rice croquettes filled with buffalo-milk cheese, which dangles around the chin like a telephone cord when bitten
- *Gnocchi alla Romana*—semolina flour boiled in milk with Parmesan and beaten eggs and then baked in the oven. (When made with mashed potatoes, gnocchi is insipid. Gnocco in the singular means pudding-head.)
- *Fettuccine al burro*—tagliatelle served with grated cheese and lashings of butter
- *Zuppa d'Arzilla*—soup made of a muddy-tasting fish from the mouth of the Tiber, lampreys and octopus. (In Rome, *brodetto* stands for lamb broth with egg yolks.)
- *Stracciatella* (little rags)—hot consommé with a thin batter of eggs which splits up into little tatters (also an ice cream flavour)
- *Melanzane al forno*—slices of aubergine, tomato and cheese baked in the oven. Served in an earthenware container, it is practically a meal in itself.
- *Carciofi alla romana*—artichokes cooked in a casserole with mint leaves and garlic
- *Insalata di misticanza*—fennel, tomatoes, radishes and *misticanza*, a plant known in English as rocket. (Romans say it takes four people to make a salad properly: a philosopher to season it, a miser to put in the vinegar, a big spender for the oil and a madman to toss it.)

ROMAN WINES

Rome's favourite wines are the Castelli Romani vintages from the Alban hills, and Frascati in particular. Always white, Frascati comes in distinctive narrow bottles in dry, *amabile* (semi-sweet) and *cannelino* (sweet) varieties.

Marino, from around Castel Gandolfo, is considered the best, especially when served directly from the barrel. The red Cesanese wines from Frosinone are also popular.

For foreigners, the best known wine in Lazio is Est! Est!! Est!!! because of its name. The story goes that on his way

to Rome in 1110, a German Cardinal called Johann Fugger sent his steward ahead to scout for inns where the wine was good, with instructions to chalk 'Est' (it is) on the door. At Montefiascone he found the man dead drunk in front of a tavern on whose door was scrawled Est! Est!! Est!!! The cardinal did such justice to Montefiascone wine that he was buried there. You can still see the inscription on his tombstone in the churchyard of San Flaviano which runs, in Latin: 'It is. It is. Because too much of it is here Jo Defuk (the stonecutter's spelling was weak) my lord is dead.'

DINING ETIQUETTE

Here are a few basic points to be considered if you are invited to an Italian home or at a restaurant as a guest among a company larger than one-to-one.

- Sit where you are placed.
- Keep both your forearms on the table but not your elbows.

- If you have several glasses and pieces of silverware in front of you, don't panic. It simply means 'a lot of food'. Like everywhere, you start from the outside and work inwards. For glasses, you'll be served. If not, keep the basic two: larger glass for the water and smaller one for the wine. If there is a huge glass, there will be a very special wine served.
- Don't start before your host or hostess.
- If you're served from a tray, when you have enough on your plate say *"Basta grazie"* ("Enough, thank you.")
- If you need something that is out of reach, say *"Posso avere del pane per favore"* ("May I have some bread please.") or ask the waiter directly.
- Italians talk about food while they are eating. If you enjoy something, you may say something like *"E' buonissimo!"* ("It's excellent!").
- Mobile phones should be turned off at all times.
- Find a way to exchange at least a few words with the person on your right and on your left, as well as with your

Due to Italy's fine weather, outdoor cafés are a common sight. Despite the more relaxed mood of the setting, dining etiquette still applies.

host and hostess. If necessary, prepare a few questions to ask beforehand.

- If you have to leave the table during the meal, say *"Scusatemi"* ("Please excuse me."). You have to explain in detail what you are going to do out of the room.
- Stand from your seat when your host or hostess does.
- Taking leave you may say *"Grazie per l'ottima cena e per la squisita compagnia"* ("Thank you for the excellent dinner and the delightful company.")

ENJOYING THE CULTURE

CHAPTER 7

'Lump the whole thing! Say that the Creator
made Italy from designs by Michael Angelo!'
—Mark Twain

ARCHITECTURE

According to UNESCO, over 50 per cent of the world's great works of art are to be found in Italy. This staggering statistic is backed by a lengthy tradition. Three thousand years ago, the so-called Villanovan culture was producing small yet beautiful objects. But the first great artistic impulse came when Hellenic migrants colonised most of the south and the Etruscans settled in the centre of the peninsula, well before the foundation of Rome.

Forming a loose confederation of city states perched on strategic points between the Tiber and the Arno, the Etruscans developed the region's mineral wealth and brought more than a whiff of the Orient to Tuscany. The markets of Etruria were flooded with products from the East—gold, silver, ivory, precious stones, jewellery, decorated ostrich egg-shells, blue-glazed Egyptian earthenware—which Phoenician ships conveyed across the Mediterranean in exchange for Etruscan iron ore, copper, tin, zinc and other metals.

The Etruscans wore oriental robes and Hellenic sandals and bonnets. They used the royal insignia of Lydia, cultivated the eastern art of soothsaying and constructed vaulted tombs like those in ancient Egypt. Often carved out of rock, these tombs are filled with murals depicting banquets, dances and athletic contests, which give us glimpses of how they lived.

If little remains of Etruscan cities beyond some massive encircling walls and a few monumental arched gateways, it is because the buildings and even the temples were constructed of wood and terracotta tiles.

The Greeks, however, built grandly in durable stone, and some of the finest examples of their architecture are to be seen at Paestum (now Pesto), Agrigento, Segesta and Selinus. Linked by trade with the homeland across the sea, Magna Graecia (the ancient Greek seaports in the south of Italy) was a storehouse from which Hellenic products were distributed by ship all along the Tuscan coast. The Greeks gave the Etruscans their alphabet, their mythological figures, their legends and their art.

The Roman Period

By contrast, the more down-to-earth Romans were slow to develop their artistic talents. For centuries they were content to import Greek works of art and commission Etruscans to design their temples. As late as the second century BC, Roman art was essentially functional. Sculpture served official

Ancient and modern buildings line the banks of the Tiber River in Rome. The dome of St Peter's is in the background.

purposes; it was only subsequently that a more plastic style began to evolve.

Early Roman architecture was concerned with defensive walls, aqueducts and public works. Private houses were straightforward, unadorned structures, built round a central atrium which served to collect rainwater. (That this basic design hardly changed over the centuries illustrates the self-contained nature of the average Roman family.)

Using the Etruscan rounded arch, the Romans erected triumphal gateways and grandiose basilicas for political gatherings. Their amphitheatres employed the technique of superimposing layers of doric, ionic and corinthian columns—the Colosseum, inaugurated in 80 BC, is a prime example. They went in for triumphal columns to display their war trophies.

Characteristic of Rome's urban architecture are the 10 bridges across the Tiber and the gateways flanked by towers which look like fortresses. As in every Roman city, life in the capital centred round the Forum—a *piazza* flanked by porticoes and public buildings in which the people assembled.

One of the oldest and most evocative is the Forum at Pompeii, a great rectangular expanse surrounded on three sides by double colonnades, with the Temple of Jupiter at its head. Of the imperial palaces, only traces of six remain. But the best-preserved, Diocletian's at Split (Spalato) in Croatia, is a good example of late Roman architecture. Rectangular in shape, it is enclosed by high walls. The three entrances are defended by towers, and inside four square buildings are grouped round a temple. To all intents and purposes, this grim palace might be a military camp.

Scattered around Italy and what was once the Roman Empire you will find the ruins of theatres, thermal sites, stadiums, swimming baths, aqueducts and so forth, testifying to the Romans' passion for solid civic constructions. Many Italian towns were built on Roman foundations.

Their sculpture was mainly statuary, for the imperial epoch loved bronzes and marbles—indeed some 140 heads of Augustus have survived. At the time of the Antonines, drills

Historical buildings attract many visitors all year round.

were used to sculpt the hairstyle and give a more intense expression to the eyes.

Painting came into fashion in the second century BC, usually as murals for public buildings and private dwellings. Little of it remains and the best examples of Roman artwork are to be found at Pompeii and Herculaneum.

What has weathered the centuries better are the famous Roman mosaic floors, which even now are being unearthed. Mosaics were also used to decorate walls and vaulted ceilings —at Ravenna, for example.

Christian Art

The earliest Christians were buried in catacombs instead of being cremated in the Roman manner, and it was there that Christian art began to emerge, largely adapted from existing traditions.

The first churches were modelled on pagan temples, with a portico in each wall and a font in the middle. The central nave was reserved for the clerics, who had the men to their right and the women on their left. The altar and the episcopal chair stood in a semi-circular apse; beneath the apse was a crypt containing the relic of a martyr which could be seen through a small opening.

In addition, there were circular mausoleums and baptistries, also derived from pagan shrines, their chief characteristic being that all points on the perimeter should be equidistant from the centre, and covered by a cupola.

By convention the Byzantine period starts with Justinian's recapture of Ravenna in AD 540, but actually the great monuments in that city date from different periods.

Shaped like a Roman cross, the mausoleum of Galla Placidia (the glamorous princess who governed the Empire so improvidently) and the Orthodox Baptistry, erected on the old Roman baths, date from the fifth century. The Arian Baptistry and Theodoric's mausoleum were built at the turn of the century; the octagonal Church of San Vitale was consecrated in AD 547.

All are Byzantine in style and decorated with mystical, colourful mosaics that are the most glorious expression

Contrast of cultures at the Piazza dei Popolo in Rome:
an obelisk from ancient Egypt is crowned with a cross.

of early Christian art, surpassing even those of Venice and Constantinople.

Romanesque Art

The decline of the feudal system and the birth of the free communes opened up the way for trade. With the growth of urban centres came a new type of rich burghers along with a host of artisans whose native talents produced a new type of art. This is known as Romanesque.

The purest examples of Romanesque architecture are to be found in Lombardy and Emilia (St Ambrogio at Milan, San Michele at Pavia, the Cathedral of Modena).

Elsewhere, regional influences prevailed. In the Veneto, the Romanesque style tended to merge with the Byzantine: at St Mark's, for example, the Byzantine cupola and decorations are set off by a façade of Romanesque arches.

Tuscan architecture was characterised by a purity of line and simplicity of decoration which made great use of coloured marble.

In the south and in Sicily, Romanesque architecture shows the exuberant influence of Byzantine, Arab and Norman tastes in its interplay of cupolas, horseshoe arches, slender campaniles and colourful decorations.

A special feature of the Romanesque period was the cloister, dedicated to monastic meditation. But apart from religious buildings there was also an increase in civic architecture—municipal *palazzi* and private mansions. Towns were fortified by encircling walls, traces of which still remain, though they have often been incorporated into later structures. In painting, there were two different trends: the Venetian, which followed the more abstract Byzantine tradition, and the Lombard, which displayed a more realistic taste.

Meanwhile, in monasteries all over the country, dedicated amanuenses were producing exquisite illuminated manuscripts of the classical texts.

13th-century Painting

Towards the end of the 13th century, however, Cimabue and Giotto virtually re-invented painting. In a series of remarkable

Crucifixions, Cimabue portrayed Christ as a triumphant figure vanquishing death, rather than oppressed by his sufferings. This was a turning point in pictorial representation, and since Giotto was his pupil, both are credited with the introduction of a new and more naturalistic style.

A new style also marked the churches that were being built in Florence by the great orders (S. Maria Novella, the Annunziata, Ognissanti, S. Spirito, Santà Croce). But the most ambitious project was the Duomo. It was built under the supervision of Arnolfo di Cambio (in the presence of Dante) and only crowned a hundred years later with Brunelleschi's unique cupola.

Secular art was developing too. Architecturally both the Palazzo Vecchio and the Bargello displayed a firm rhythm and a well-defined shape. It seemed that Giotto's influence was to be found everywhere—certainly the art of Andrea Pisano, who came to Florence to cast the Baptistry doors, matched his elegant verve. Above all Giotto's dramatic power was shown in the frescos he painted at Padua and Assisi.

Yet Duccio di Buoninsegna (1255-1318), the first great Sienese painter, used his experience with miniatures to blend Byzantine and Gothic styles. His superb craftsmanship—the rich subtle colours and the use of gold—was to characterise the Sienese school for the following two centuries.

Gothic Art

If the Gothic style was basically a French import, in Italy it took on a more classic flavour, modifying the Romanesque spirit to meet religious and secular needs. At the same time, it marked the artisan's emancipation to that of an artist who endowed his work with a personal identity.

Milan Cathedral is often considered to be the paragon of Gothic art. Begun in 1386 and completed only in the 19th century, it displays a variety of features—the façade alone contains Gothic embrasures, rectangular windows from the 14th century and a central loggia in Napoleonic style.

Other Gothic examples are the Cathedral of S. Andrea at Vercelli, the Baptistry at Parma, the unfinished building of Siena Cathedral (which was abandoned because of the plague), the Cathedral of Orvieto and the Duomo in Florence.

During the Gothic period, artists strove for greater realism and purity of form. In the first half of the 14th century, Tuscan painting was supreme: the two great schools were those of Florence and Siena.

In Florence, Giotto was succeeded by Maso di Banco, Bernardo Daddi and Taddeo Gaddi. In Siena, Simone Martini and the Lorenzetti brothers followed Duccio's lead, yet were aware of Giotto. Thus there was a stylistic link between the two schools.

In most towns and cities, municipal buildings were erected to rival the cathedrals, such as the Ducal Palace in Venice and the Palazzi Communali in Piacenza and Siena.

The Quattrocento

This was the century that saw the triumph of humanism in Florence. Reacting against Gothic conventions, its artists sought to recapture the classical spirit. They no longer regarded art as a manual activity, but as an expression of the intellect. Nature had to be seen objectively in all its beauty, history viewed as a continuous process of transformation. For them, culture reflected communal life. So great was the relationship between the arts that the painter could be an architect as well as a man of ideas; the philosopher could be an artist.

These are some of the leading figures of the 15th century, most of them Tuscans:

- Having begun his career in Florence with a contest to sculpt the Baptistry doors, Filippo Brunelleschi (1377–1446) studied the laws of perspective and methods of construction in classical Rome. He was concerned with urban planning, the balance between buildings and landscape.

  In Florence he designed the Church of San Lorenzo for the Medici in 1418, the Ospedale degli Innocenti, the Pazzi chapel and the Church of Santo Spirito. But his crowning achievement was the magnificent cupola of the Duomo, which required 14 years of work and was completed in 1434.

- As philosopher, theoretician and architect, Leon Battista Alberti (1404–1472) was the principal exponent of humanism. His treatises on sculpture, painting and architecture became a recognised rationale of the whole movement. Alberti believed that sculpture and painting should cease being purely decorative and strike out on their own. He distinguished two different trends in the return to classicism: the Hellenic tradition expressed by artists such as the della Robbias and Ghiberti, and the Roman tradition represented by Donatello. The Malatesta temple at Rimini, the Palazzo Rucellai and the projected façade for Santa Maria Novella in Florence, as well as the Church of S. Andrea at Mantua demonstrate his own architectural ideals.

- Lorenzo Ghiberti (1378–1455) believed that perspective should be a means of stylistic expression rather than an artistic imperative. Though he made his mark as sculptor, goldsmith and writer, his most important achievement was the doors of the Baptistry at Florence. Ghiberti established a large workshop to make these doors, and his atelier was the principal training ground for the next generation of artists, such as Donatello, Masolino and Uccello.

- Luca della Robbia (1400–1482), the head of a famous family of Florentine potters, perfected the technique for glazing terracotta. This remained unsurpassed, and the family's work secrets were never known outside the shop.

  The hallmark of Luca's ceramics, which adorned the chantry of Florence Cathedral, Giotto's campanile and many other churches, was an ivory white foreground on a light blue background, executed in a suave, almost reticent style. His nephew Andrea della Robbia (1435–1525) introduced more grace and colour to the range. His celebrated majolicas—to be found at Arezzo, Siena, Prato, Pistoia, Città di Castello as well as Florence—can be recognised by their subtle use of green and yellow in the background.

- Arguably the greatest Florentine sculptor before Michelangelo, Donatello (1386–1466) was certainly the most individual artist of the 15th century. Like his friend Brunelleschi, he was a humanist, but in a different way. Whereas Brunelleschi's interpretation of humanism was rational and intellectual, Donatello's rendering was naturalistic and exuberant, yet with a respect for the past.

  This combination gave his work grandeur and originality. The *St John the Baptist* (1415), *St George* (1416) and *David* (1440) are astonishing masterpieces of his bold and forceful style. Much of the later 15th-century painting stems from him, as does the whole of the Paduan school; while through Mantegna and Bellini his influence was felt even in Venice.

- In painting Masaccio (1401–1428) founded the so-called 'heroic style'. Severity has always been the dominant trait of the Florentine genius, and Masaccio's austere rendering of the human body had a determining effect on later artists.

Italy is full of historical artefacts and sculptures. Here, someone makes a point at the Palazzo del Conservatori in Rome.

The true predecessor of Leonardo and Michelangelo, he painted the figures of the *Acts of the Apostles* as heroic, rugged personages arranged in a strictly controlled space and lit by a constant fall of light—his purpose being to achieve realism by subordinating the composition to an almost geometric perspective and illumination.

- Paolo Uccello (1397–1475) began by helping Ghiberti with the doors of the Florentine Baptistry, then worked with Donatello on the mosaics of St Mark's at Venice and at Padua. His paintings are distinguished by such a fantastic, almost surrealist, sense of perspective—as in the *St George and the Dragon*, and the *Battle of San Romano* series—that they have been regarded as the forerunners of contemporary trends, from Cubism to Surrealism.

- Piero della Francesca (1415–1492) was one of the greatest artists of a great century. His stories of the Cross, frescoed in Arezzo, transform a legend into spectacular liturgical action. *The Pregnant Madonna* in the tiny chapel at Monterchi unites human truth and mystery; the *Resurrection of Christ at S. Sepolcro* emanates a reverberating force; the *Dittico of Urbino* celebrates individual humanity and dignity.

- Sandro Botticelli (1445–1510) had a rapid and brilliant career. At the age of 25, he already had his own atelier. Philosophic, religious and moral problems haunted his paintings; indeed his mythological pictures—*Primavera and The Birth of Venus*—have allegorical and Christianising messages. Often his style seems deliberately archaic. In 1481–1482 he was in Rome painting frescos in the Sistine Chapel along with Ghirlandaio, Cosimo Rosselli and Perugino.

- Ghirlandaio (1449–1494) was the best fresco exponent of his generation. The naturalistic detail he put into his paintings, which followed the fashion of the day, made him immensely popular. The *bottega* he set up with his two brothers (and with Michelangelo as an apprentice) catered for a rising mercantile clientele; moreover his practice of introducing portraits of local notables into religious scenes meant that there was practically no church in Florence without at least one of his altarpieces.

- Pinturicchio (1454–1513) worked with Perugino on the Borgia apartments at the Vatican and collaborated with Raphael on the story of Pius II in the Piccolomini Library at Siena. Prolonging the fashion for rich, picturesque art, he became the head of a workshop which specialised in precious and often bizarre effects. The first to use 'grotesques' to frame fairy-like and noble scenes, his paintings had an attractive, light-hearted charm.

- Mantegna (1431–1506) became the court painter at Mantua, where he decorated the Camera degli Sposi, a masterpiece of *trompe-l'oeil* perspective. The 'antiquarian' of the Quattrocento, he depicted religious themes against a background of Roman history— gnarled figures moving through rocky backgrounds in a blue-grey light. It was through him that the Germans, particularly Dürer, discovered Italy, antiquity and the Renaissance.

- After training in Naples, Antonello (1430–1479) went to Milan and then Venice, where the impact of northern piety on his southern taste for plasticity, led him to take an increasing interest in the human face. His *Ecce Homo* became the ultimate image of human distress; and by treating his pictures as a continuation of real space (like a chapel opening out of a church) he drew spectators into the scene.

The Cinquecento

In the 16th century (or *Cinquecento* as the Italians call it) the High Renaissance extended and developed humanistic concepts. Despite political upheavals—foreign invasions and economic crisis—artistic life became stronger, more worldly and less spiritual.

Archeological discoveries gave a boost to classical enquiry, though later in the century there was a contrary reaction in the shape of Mannerism—a term often used disparagingly, but which at the time meant a desire to cut loose from medieval mythology. The names most famously associated with this period are:

- Leonardo da Vinci (1452–1519) marks the beginning of the High Renaissance. The prototype of the 'universal man', Leonardo was not only one of the greatest Italian artists but anticipated many later breakthroughs in anatomy, aeronautics, engineering and other domains. He left thousands of drawings, but only a handful of paintings. If his early paintings were inspired by a desire to surprise and fascinate, the *non-finito*, or rough sketch, became more important for him than the finished work.

  The intellectual powers which enabled him to master 'hard and dry matter' (as Vasari called it) were so diffused that he brought hardly any major enterprise to a conclusion. Nevertheless he gave fresh life to portraiture and landscape, developing a *sfumato* technique which merged contours and background, so that the sea-green atmosphere which characterised his paintings merged into the blue distance.

  After a period in Florence where he produced the *Baptism* and *Annunciation* (which are now in the Uffizi), the portrait of Ginevra Benci, the *Madonna Benois* and the *Adoration of the Magi*, Leonardo moved to Milan where he painted the *Virgin of The Rocks*, the frescos in the Castello Sforzesco and the *Last Supper* in the refectory of Santa Maria delle Grazie.

  Returning to Florence in 1503, he did a great deal of dissection and worked on various artistic projects. The most important was a commission shared with Michelangelo (whom he disliked) for two huge frescos to commemorate Florentine victories. Leonardo's was the *Battle of Anghiari*, which he did in some wax medium copied from an antique technique. This failed, and the paintings was the celebrated portrait of *La Gioconda*, done at Vignamaggio, Mona Lisa Gherardini's home in Chianti.

- Michelangelo Buonarroti (1475–1564) whose long career was divided between Florence and Rome—alternating painting with sculpture and architecture —exemplifies the fecundity of genius and its spiritual drama.

Born at Caprese, Michelangelo was apprenticed to Ghirlandaio before joining the school set up in the Medici gardens by Lorenzo. When the Medici were expelled, he went to Rome where he sculpted the *Bacchus* (now in the Bargello) and the intricate St Peter's *Pietà*, whose formal perfection made him famous.

Returning to Florence in 1501, he carved the great *David* as well as the *Piccolomini* altarpiece in Siena Cathedral, and began to fresco the *Battle of Cascina* in the Signoria. His most important work was the ceiling of the Sistine Chapel. Its heroic quality changed the whole rend of painting and earned him the sobriquet of *il divino Michelangelo*.

Next, Michelangelo sculpted the remarkable tombs in the new Sacristy and designed the Laurenziana Library in Florence. After the Medici were again expelled, he supervised the fortifications of San Miniato and the area south of the city in Chianti. Recalled to Rome, where he spent the last 30 years of his life, Michelangelo frescoed the *Last Judgement* on the altar wall of the Sistine Chapel.

At the age of 75, he bade farewell to painting, wrote his best poetry and carved the *Pietà* in the Duomo in Florence. He was still chipping at his last work—the nearly abstract *Rondanini Pietà*—a few days before he died at the age of 90.

- Better known as Raphael, Raffaello Sanzio (1483–1520), whose personal charm and career fascinated his contemporaries, was the son of a court painter at Urbino. After working with Perugino in Perugia, Raphael moved to Florence where he assimilated the techniques of Leonardo and Michelangelo.

Having painted a number of *Madonnas* (which are now in the Uffizi and the Pitti), he soon came to be regarded as their equal and was employed at the Vatican, where Michelangelo was painting the Sistine Chapel. There, Raphael decorated the Stanza della Segnatura. The theme was human intellect and his two serene, classically balanced frescos representing

Philosophy and Theology are supreme examples of the High Renaissance.

By then at the peak of his career, Raphael took over from Bramante as the architect of St Peter's, and painted the frescos at the Villa Farnesina as well as a series of Old Testament scenes for the loggia of the Vatican. He also designed tapestries for the Sistine Chapel and during the last seven years of his life produced a number of masterpieces governed by what contemporaries called *mirabile giudizio*—the power to express characters through drawing.

- Giorgio Vasari (1511–1574), who spent a busy and productive life painting in Rome and Florence, also wrote the *Lives of the Artists*. By chronicling what happened from the days of Cimabue and Giotto until his own time, he is the most valuable (and entertaining) source on the development of Italian art.

- Another notable figure was Andrea Palladio (1508–1580) who gave his name to a style of architecture which inspired many imitators (including Inigo Jones who started English 'palladianism'). Fascinated by the stateliness and the proportions of ancient Rome, Palladio kept to a classical style but introduced innovations which lightened the aspect and created more space.

In Vincenzo, he designed a number of fine buildings, including the Palazzo della Ragione with its open arcades, the Barbarano, Porti and Chieregati *palazzi* and the Teatro Olimpico. He also conceived many country houses, of which the best known are the Villa Capri and the Villa Barbaro at Maser. In Venice, too, he built several stately churches, such as the famous San Giorgio Maggiore, and various large *palazzi* on the Grand Canal.

The Seicento

Seventeenth-century artists laboured under the shadow of the Counter-Reformation and were obliged to follow the dictates of the Council of Trent. With less liberty of expression, they tended to choose religious subjects. Since Rome was the centre of patronage, the ground rules were laid down by the Papacy and represented the culture and the politics of the Church. It was the period of the Baroque.

Yet two pictorial genres emerged which had a profound effect on Italian culture: the classical style of the Carracci family, and the naturalistic school of Caravaggio.

There were three Carraccis, all from Bologna: Ludovico and his cousins Agostino and Annibale, who were brothers. Together they founded the Accademia degli Incamminati at Rome which encouraged young painters to move from Mannerism to Baroque.

Annibale Carracci (1560–1609) was the best artist of the three. In 1595, he went to Rome to work on the Farnese Palace. The famous Galleria with its mythological frescos, open colonnade and nude figures reminiscent of the Sistine ceiling, ranks as one of the great pieces of Italian painting. It has a lightness of touch, a sense of humour and a freshness of vision that were to influence European decoration.

Radically opposed to the new ideas expressed by the Carraccis was Caravaggio (1571–1610) with his vivid realism, his use of contemporary costumes and settings, his handling of light. He was the master of *chiaroscuro*. Almost black opaque shadows were contrasted with equally strong lights. For realism he made a point of introducing common people into his religious scenes.

Caravaggio's reputation as a scandalous reprobate given to brawls, duels, ill-treatment of prostitutes and outrageous behaviour towards some of his fellow painters came to a head when he stabbed his opponent at a game of tennis and fled to Malta. There, falling foul of an official, he was imprisoned but escaped to Sicily where he did some paintings in Syracuse and Messina.

His end is obscure. At Naples he was attacked by cut-throats and left for dead. Fleeing in a sailing boat, he reached Porto Ercole on the Tuscan coast, was imprisoned by mistake, and released only to find that the boat had already left with all his belongings aboard. He died, maybe of rage or perhaps of malaria, on 18 July 1610. A maverick, to be sure. Nevertheless his paintings were to dominate much of the century.

The Settecento

As France developed into the centre of European culture, the focal point of Italian art moved north to Venice, and Baroque gave way to a new style known as Rococo.

Graceful and sophisticated, Rococo was admirably suited for interior decoration. It inspired minor arts such as furniture and porcelain, and provoked a vogue for painting romantic ruins.

Giambattista Tiepolo (1696–1770), who headed a busy group of Venetian artists, was the purest exponent of Italian Rococo and the greatest decorator of the 18th century. His style was light and loose. The frescos in the Archbishop's Palace at Udine show his virtuosity in handling pale colours to create a world in steep perspective, receding giddily into the distance.

An illustrious contemporary was Canaletto (1697–1768), whose father painted theatre sets in Venice. After working with him as a boy, Canaletto went to Rome and began painting townscapes as souvenirs for tourists. In 1720, he moved to Florence, where he found a ready market for these *vedute* among the English residents. His *vedute* were precise and full of harmony, their little figures drawn with great vivacity.

If Rococo was all the rage in the earlier part of the century, a Neoclassical movement took over in the second half. There was a reaction against the pomposity of Baroque and the bizarre affectations of Rococo. Artists gave up copying nature in favour of what they chose to consider beautiful, without memorable success.

Canova (1757–1822) became the most famous Neoclassical sculptor. Trained as a mason, he already had his own studio in Venice at the age of 17. The French invasion caused him to leave for Vienna, however, where he was commissioned to sculpt a monument for Maria Christina in the Augustiner Kirsche. In 1802, prompted by the Vatican, he accepted Napoleon's invitation to go to Paris and carve a bust of him from life.

> **Napoleon's Works**
>
> Canova's best-known works are the portrait of Napoleon's sister Pauline as Venus, and the monuments to Clement XIII and Clement XIV in Rome. It was he who conceived the idea of incorporating the tomb, like a simplified pyramid, into the design of a sculptured memorial.

After the fall of Napoleon, Canova was sent by the Pope to Paris to try and get back the art treasures looted by the French. Thanks to English help he was largely successful and was made Marchese d'Ischia. A kindly man, he spent most of his large fortune helping young students.

Mention should also be made of Giuseppe Piermarini (1734–1808) who carried out the urban planning of Milan and designed the Teatro alla Scala, the paradigm of Italian opera houses.

19th Century

During the first part of the century Italian art was derivative, imitating the vogues that were current abroad, and of very little merit. For the record, there were numerous groups of artists:

- The Nazarenes, formed in Rome by students from the Vienna Academy, proposed a return to medieval values, but with spiritual and religious liberty.
- The Purists aimed to retrieve the technique of the Old Masters.
- The Pre-Raphaelites wanted to antedate Raphael and emulate the *Quattrocento*, even to the point of turning painters into artisans.
- The Neo-Gothics proposed a return to medieval art and Lombard architecture.
- The Romantics were inspired by medieval and *Risorgimento* ideals—which in the case of Francesco Hayez (1791–1882) made for some good portraits of women and displayed a clever use of colours.

In Italy, famous buildings have been preserved
and offer an insight into Italy's long history.

As the century wore on, painting became regionalised and infused with local traditions. But gradually the Impressionists made some headway, especially in Lombardy.

Venetian artists continued with their *vedute* and scenes of everyday life.

Tuscan painters were influenced by the Macchiaioli (or daubers), the most significant artistic movement of the period. The Macchiaioli's technique lay in destroying static shapes and reconstructing them by means of splashes of colour rather than lineal drawings.

By contrast, the Divisionists worked on the principle that colours should be painted directly on the canvas and not mixed in the palette, the theory being that the viewer's eye would do the job.

On the other hand, Giuseppe Pellizza da Volpedo (1868–1907) conveyed a social message. His *Quarto Stato*, which hangs in Milan, is considered to be the pictorial manifesto of Italian socialism.

20th Century

This century inherited two artistic trends: on the one hand, Realism; on the other, Decadence. The realists sought to portray a society in full transformation; the decadents looked inwards at its effect on the human soul.

Throughout Europe there were new radical movements, which varied in different countries. In Italy the emergence of abstract art was known as Futurism, Metaphysic painting and Surrealism. A breakaway, controversial group were the Dadaists.

These avant-garde movements dispersed between the two world wars, when the political and economic situation in Europe was hardly conducive to cultural exchanges or the circulation of new ideas.

There were a few local schools in Italy, but the ideology of the Fascist regime predominated and many artists emigrated to the United States.

After the second conflict, the impact of technological and industrial expansion on American lines saw the emergence

Why not do something a bit different and get your portrait painted by a street artist, like this one outside Uffizi Gallery in Florence?

of artistic phenomena such as *l'informale*, conceptual art, MAC, pop art, *l'arte povera* and *transavanguardia*.

The futurists, whose aims date back to a manifesto of 1909, sought to restore the *élan* of national art and overcome the provincialism that had bedevilled Italian painting for over a century. By depicting the tensions and speed of urban life they hoped to revolutionise the concept of pictorial expression. To achieve this they relied on the abstract use of pure colour. In the belief that painting should interpret reality rather than portray physical experience, they opted for total freedom of composition and chromatic effects to a point where the viewer was left bewildered and even troubled.

The most influential Italian artists of the 20th century have been Giorgio de Chirico (1888–1978), who founded the Metaphysic movement, and Amedeo Modigliani (1884–1920), who is best known for his female nudes.

MUSIC

Italy's musical heritage is immemorial. After all, music was part of Etruscan culture, accompanying almost every religious and social activity. Skilful flautists helped hunters to catch game which, as if drawn by the power of their melodies, fell into the nets.

Part of the early church music has survived in the lovely liturgies of Palestrina (1525–1594) who was the first in a long line of distinguished composers such as Albinoni, Vivaldi, the Scarlattis, Cherubini and Paganini.

Most people, however, associate Italian music with opera, which started in Florence towards the end of the 16th century as a musical representation of Greek tragedy. In 1637, the first opera house opened in Venice. But Naples soon emerged as the chief centre of opera, which initially tended to be comic, singing the songs of the street.

Although Peri's *Euridice* was the earliest real opera, Claudio Monteverdi (1567–1643), the highly accomplished composer of sacred and secular music, is generally considered to be opera's founding father. By mixing *bel canto* and *buffo* styles with dramatic speech, Monteverdi set the model for generations to come.

Briefly, the other great names are:

- Lulli (often spelt Lully), a Florentine who became the master of music at the court of Louis XIV and collaborated with Molière to produce opera-ballets aimed at glorifying the French monarch.

- Rossini (1792–1868), who composed florid and showy music for the greatest voices of the age to sing. His irresistible melodies and energetic rhythm, coupled with a splendid sense of humour, made his operas popular all over Europe. Works such as Tancred, The Barber of Seville and William Tell earned him the epithet 'Napoleon of Music'.

- Donizetti (1797–1848), who broke the tradition of the happy ending. Lucia di Lammermoor, based on Scott's novel, consolidated his international acclaim.

- Bellini (1801–1835), who demonstrated more delicacy and refinement. His Norma, a great lyric drama, and La Sonnambula, a rustic idyll, influenced both Chopin and Berlioz.

- Verdi (1813–1901), who was associated with the Risorgimento—his operas were seen as gestures for liberty and his name became an acrostic: Viva Verdi meant Viva Vittorio Emanuele Re D'Italia. Verdi's talent was remarkable. He had a flair for startling situations and dramatic stage effects; his tunes were so catchy that barrel organs churned them out. Verdi ranks as the greatest Italian composer of opera.

  His best-known works are Ernani, based on Victor Hugo's Hernani; Rigoletto, based on Hugo's play Le Roi S'Amuse; Il Trovatore, based on a Spanish drama by Gatteerez; La Traviata, after Dumas' play La Dame aux Camélias; Un Ballo in Maschera, based on Auber's Le Bal Masqué; Aida, composed for the opening of the Suez Canal; Otello and Falstaff, drawn from Shakespeare's plays.

- Mascagni and Leoncavallo are noted for two one-act operas. So often are Mascagni's Cavalleria Rusticana and Leoncavallo's Pagliacci featured together on the programme that they are known to opera buffs as 'Cav

You don't have to spend money to enjoy cultural performances. Street musicians and marching bands can provide high-quality entertainment at no cost.

and Pag'. Subsequently Mascagni became the musical mouthpiece of fascist Italy and died disgraced in hotel in Rome; while sadly Leoncavallo never recaptured the grand manner of his single great opera.

- Puccini (1858–1924) was born at Lucca and was a fellow pupil of Mascagni's. His favourite theme was the woman who loved too much. In La Bohème she is Mimi, a dress-maker's assistant; in Manon Lescaut she is a prostitute; in Madama Butterfly a Japanese geisha; in Tosca a singer; in Turandot the little slave girl Liu. With Puccini the great days of Italian opera ended.

Cultural Performances

A wide variety of cultural activities—music, theatre, the arts —takes place in Italy all year round.

Each region, city and even village has an *assessore alla cultura* (culture council member) and his office, the *Assessorato*, will be able to give you details of forthcoming events. So will the local tourist office (APT).

Many of the performances are renowned throughout the world. Don't miss them if you happen to be in the area at the right time.

Here are just a few:

- The Festival Dei Due Mondi at Spoleto for avant-garde music and theatre.
- The Film Festival at Venice for movies.
- The Biennale di Venezia for contemporary art (held every other year).
- The opera season in most large towns—notably Milan, Parma, Florence, Rome and Naples.
- Spectacular operatic performances in evocative settings are held in the Roman Arena at Verona, the Terme di Caracalla in Rome, the Sferistero at Macerata and at Taormina's Greek theatre.

The dress code for these events is like everywhere else in Europe. A good rule of thumb is to dress in accordance with the formality of the occasion and the price of your ticket.

For instance, a first night at the Scala in Milan calls for black tie and long gown, except in the *loggione* (or 'god's') where more casual clothes are common. Even so, shorts and T-shirts would hardly be appropriate.

LITERATURE

Italian literature was born in the 13th century when a group of poets at Frederick II's court began to write in the vernacular. After the emperor's death, these literati converged on Florence, where a flourishing school of poetry grew up, and Dante Alighieri emerged as the first great literary figure.

Dante's *Divine Comedy* was written in the Tuscan idiom, and since many Italians can quote whole chunks (and frequently do), one should at least know the gist of it for social occasions.

The Divine Comedy

With matchless rhythm and profoundly beautiful imagery, Dante tells the story of a sinful man's journey through hell and purgatory, before finally reaching the highest point of heaven where he sees God. His guide through hell is Virgil, a symbol of reason. Together they descend down a funnel-shaped abyss which contains the souls of the damned in 10 successive circles. The lower they get, the more wicked are the sinners, and Virgil explains the reasons why they are there.

At the bottom is Satan, frozen to his waist in ice, and gnawing with three dreadful mouths the arch traitors: Judas, who betrayed Christ, along with Brutus and Cassius who betrayed Julius Caesar.

Emerging from hell, Dante and Virgil start climbing the seven hills of Mount Purgatory, each cliff of which represents a cardinal sin. But here the atmosphere brightens because, once purged of their transgressions, these souls can hope to reach heaven.

Near the top, Virgil disappears and Beatrice (as the symbol of divine faith) guides him through the constellation of moon, planets and stars to the beatific vision.

A wine shop in Tuscany. The vineyards in Italy produce a range of high quality wine and meals are often enjoyed with a glass of wine.

Italian cafes are great places to unwind and to soak in the beauty and romance of the country.

The entrance to an apartment in a small neighbourhood. Opposite page: The Duomo (Duomo di Milano) in Milan is one of the world's largest churches and boasts magnificent structures and statues.

A view of the province of Trento. It is one of two provinces which make up Italy's region of Trentino-Alto Adige and is an almost entirely mountainous province with a main valley crossing its centre.

A gondolier steers a gondola through a narrow canal in Venice. The city has been known as the 'City of Water' and the 'City of Light' and is considered to be one of the most beautiful cities in the world

This magnificent medieval concept is enlivened by Dante's ironic consignment of the prominent figures of antiquity and his own day to various levels of hell or purgatory. No other literary work ever had such an impact on Italian culture or did more to establish Tuscan as the language of Italy.

Major Italian Literary Figures

Another major figure of this early period, Francesco Petrarca (Petrarch, 1304–1370) was born to Florentine parents who were exiled at the same time as Dante. But whereas Dante was essentially medieval in character, Petrarch became imbued with a spirit of Classicism.

He was proud of his Latin verse (which he boasted matched that of Virgil) and could not understand why his contemporaries preferred the poetry he wrote in Italian. This included 350 sonnets which he composed in honour of Laura, a married woman he had loved in his youth.

Although Petrarch wrote on sensuous themes, his dominant theme was the quest for self-culture and the rhythmic qualities of his verse have served European poets as a model for 500 years.

The third member of the great Florentine trio was Boccaccio (1313–1375) whose friendship with Petrarch led him to become a pioneer of humanist scholarship. His best-known work, however, is the Decameron, a collection of short stories related by a party of young men and women who had retired to a villa near Florence to escape from the plague of 1348. Distinctly permissive and highly entertaining, the stories in the Decameron were written in the new Tuscan idiom—which makes Boccaccio the father of Italian prose.

THE RENAISSANCE

The humanism pioneered by Petrarch and Boccaccio developed into the 'Revival of Learning', or in more general terms, the Renaissance.

Humanism meant the recognition of human rights and the beauty of nature. It rejected medieval values in favour of what men and women had thought and done in pre-Christian days—recalling the glories of ancient Rome.

While some authors reverted to Latin, others preferred their provincial dialects. It was largely thanks to Lorenzo de' Medici that literature was guided by Florence.

Luigi Pulci, who grew up in the Medici household, and Matteo Boiardo with his Orlando Innamorato, turned the romantic ballad into a work of art. Poliziano wrote extensively in Latin, but his masterpiece, La Giostra, was written in Tuscan and showed how successfully classical taste and learning could be grafted into the vernacular. The Sienese Pope Pius II, Aeneus Piccolomini, produced a polished and entertaining autobiography.

16TH CENTURY

The great achievement of the Renaissance between about 1494 and 1560 was that every form of art, including literature, was perfected and endowed with a classical style.

- Ludovico Ariosto (1474–1533) cultivated an elegant turn of phrase, and in Orlando Furioso (a sequel to Boiardo's Orlando Innamorato), his octave stanzas reached the highest levels of harmony and grace.

- Torquato Tasso (1544–1595) was brought up at the court in Urbino, and made his name with *Gerusalemme Liberata* (the liberation of Christ's sepulchre by Godfrey of Bouillon) which is probably the best heroic poem in Italian literature.

- The first of the great Florentine historians, Niccolo Machiavelli (1469–1527) was not only an eye-witness but also an active participant in the history of Florence. His principal works are the Istorie Fiorentine, the Arte della *Guerra* and the *Principe*—an analysis of the methods by which an ambitious man (such as Cesare Borgia) could become a successful autocrat. It was his obsession with what a state is and how to found one, that led to his reputation for 'machiavellian' duplicity. A creature of his time, 'old Nick' was colour-blind to ordinary codes of morality.

- Francesco Guicciardini (1483–1540) took up the story of Florence where Machiavelli had left off. As a diplomat and statesman, Guicciardini had played the devious game of politics, and his *Storia d'Italia* (which deals with events from the death of Lorenzo de' Medici until 1534) gives a lively insight into the motives and strategies of the European states, and the mutual jealousies of their leaders.

THE SEICENTO

After 1560, the blight of Spaniardism fell upon the land and the rot set in. Frustrated in every way, writers such as Marino, Achillini, Guidi and Testi resorted to hyperbole, useless similes and baroque words. Chiabrera showed some literary flair, but in general, 17th-century poetry was short on feeling and overlong on display.

By contrast Galileo Galilei, a great man of letters as well as of science, knew how to go straight to the point and describe complex scientific matters in a simple vernacular which could be easily understood.

THE ENLIGHTENMENT

In the 18th century conditions improved. Muratori chronicled Italian history from AD 500 to 1500. Galiani wrote on currency, Filangieri on legislation. Becciari's treatise *Dei Delitti e delle Pene* contributed to the reform of the penal system and the abolition of torture. Carlo Goldini, a Venetian, revivified the theatre by creating the comedy of character, rivalling Molière with his dramatic situations and lively dialogue. Giuseppe Parini ridiculed social pretensions, making fun of aristocratic frivolities.

The ideas current in France before the revolution—liberty, equality, a hatred of tyranny—were reflected in Italian literature. Vittorio Alfieri (1748–1803) took up the classical theme of popular liberty in arms against the tyrant. (His characters talk like modern revolutionaries.) Vincenzo Monti regarded the French Revolution as a threat to Italy, and wrote several books deploring Napoleon's victories. But being an artist, he concentrated his efforts on achieving *belle imagini, per le belle forme*. The same search for beauty marked Giambatista Niccolini's tragedies, which are lyrical rather than dramatic.

Three historians were busy as well. Carlo Betta wrote a history of Italy during the Napoleonic period, and later continued Guicciardini's history up to 1789. Piero Colletta wrote a history of Naples from 1734 to 1825, in a style borrowed from Tacitus. Lazzaro Papi's history of the French Revolution was considerably more readable than either of these.

ROMANTICISM

The reaction to this Neoclassicism (more words than feelings) was the Romantic movement (more feelings than words). It was headed by Alessandro Manzoni, whose novel *I Promessi*

Sposi is still widely read. The story is of little account, but the characters are living people with human qualities and failings.

But the most significant figure was Giacomo Leopardi, who was born at Recanati in 1798. Leopardi came from a distinguished but bigoted and avaricious family, whose domestic tyranny made him a victim of manic depression. His poems are agonising cries. But they are uttered with such high simplicity of language, and with such human appeal, that Leopardi has come to be regarded as Italy's greatest lyrical poet since Dante. He was also one of the most perfect prose writers.

RISORGIMENTO

The militant spirit which culminated in the Risorgimento gave rise to a surge of patriotic literature such as *Le mie Prigioni* by Silvio Pellico, who had been a political prisoner in Austria, and *I miei Ricordi* by Massimo D'Azeglio, who became several times prime minister.

Ippolito Nievo described the process by which Italy was united, as seen by a youthful protagonist. Apart from the poetry of Berchet and Giusti, numerous poems were written in the Milanese dialect by Carlo Porta, and in the Roman patois by Gioacchino Belli.

UNIFICATION

The major writer in the second half of the 19th century was Nobel Prize-winner Giosuè Carducci (1835–1907), whose patriotic enthusiasm soon turned into disillusionment at the way the new Italian Kingdom was being run.

In his novels, Giovanni Verga eschewed comment and let the facts speak for themselves.

Giovanni Pascoli, who succeeded Carducci at Bologna University, believed that poetry should reflect a child's sharp clarity of vision.

20TH CENTURY

Gabriele D'annunzio (1863–1938) thought just the opposite. As the leader of the 'Decadent' movement—which

Stunning scenery is part of Italy's charm. Here, two men stand at Piazza Garibaldi, Gianicolo, with a view of central Rome in the background.

echoed Dostoievsky, Tolstoy and Nietsche—he achieved a phenomenal success by sheer brilliance of style. Primitive impulses, sex and sensuousness were conveyed in an orgy of soap-opera images.

Even more eccentric was the 'futuristic' poetry of Tommaso Marinetti (1876–1944), the first writer in Italy, indeed in Europe, to advocate the need to replace bourgeois ethics by the aesthetics of the machine—the cult of speed. Italo Svevo and Nobel Prize-winner Luigi Pirandello expressed the dilemmas of contemporary life. Pirandello's characters talk endlessly but are unable to communicate with one another. 'How can we understand each other,' says one of the dramatis personae in *Six Characters in Search of an Author*, 'if in the words I use I put my own sense and values, whereas the person who is listening inevitably assumes I mean his own personal sense and values?'

> Umberto Saba was the avant-garde of a new style of poetry which projected a pan-European view (and inspired many others).

Giuseppe Ungaretti sought to achieve a concentrated, unadorned style emphasised by single words and blank spaces.

By contrast, Eugenio Montale, another Nobel Prize poet, believed in being deliberately obscure. To him the mission of poetry was to decipher the universe and promote human dignity.

FASCISM

During the Fascist period, official policy was to hark back to the grandeur of imperial Rome and to eliminate all foreign influences.

Among those who did not toe the party line were Piero Gobetti and Antonio Gramsci, who were intent on voicing left-wing attitudes—the role of the writer not being that of a censor, but of a 'technical political specialist' (i.e. linked to the proletariat).

Gobetti died in 1926. Gramsci landed up in jail. There he wrote *Quaderni dal Carcere*, which caused a literary sensation when it was published after World War II.

POST-WAR

Alberto Moravia's first offering, *Gli Indifferenti*, was acclaimed as a landmark signalling the rebirth of the Italian novel. His invariable theme was a psychological study of the corrupt world of the upper classes, through their sexual and financial shenanigans.

At the same time, there was a chorus of 'angry' young authors who depicted working-class or slum life, and the general backwardness that existed in Italy. It was, in Calvino's view, a manifold discovery of the different Italys—especially the Italys which had hitherto received little publicity in literature.

Italo Calvino (1925–1985) himself dealt with the resistance to Fascism before moving into the realms of fantastic, fairy-tale escapism. A fascination with semiotics marks his later works, the underlying motive of which is the hopelessness of describing life in urban surroundings.

Giuseppe Tomasi di Lampedusa had voiced his distrust for mankind in *Il Gattopardo*—a novel that was really out of its time, which accounts for the excitement that was caused by its discovery. The social order had to change, his main character maintained, in order that everything could stay as it was.

Another celebrated Sicilian, Leonardo Sciascia (1921–1989) denounced the Mafia in more pessimistic terms (the phenomenon of pure evil existed because men were cleverer than the devil himself).

CURRENT TRENDS

In one way or another, most leading Italian authors have become involved in film-making or script-writing, causing a special type of *intelligentsia* to grow up around Cinecitta.

Pasolini and Soldati are obvious examples. Several of the younger generation, such as Ottieri, wrote novels in the form of film scripts.

Reacting to the wave of conspicuous consumption, a coterie of purists calling themselves Gruppo 63 (their first convention was held in 1963) lashed out against the progressive commercialisation of art.

Sanguineti, Poera, Balestrini and others experimented with novels depicting humdrum daily events. No story, merely a situation.

After the revolutionary autumn of 1968, there was a move back to poetry, published in cultural reviews such as *Niebo* in Milan, *Nuovi Argomenti* in Rome and *Salvi Imprevisti* in Florence.

The past became respectable again, and the thrust was towards an uncompromisingly intellectual approach, as well as the proper use of language.

In the 1980s, literary criticism returned to the forefront, and Umberto Eco emerged as one of Italy's most incisive men of letters.

Born in Alexandria in 1932 and now Professor of Aesthetics at Bologna University, Eco first made his mark with essays on electronic music, cinema, television and European literature (including a long dissertation on James Joyce).

These were followed by studies of mass communication and popular culture—strip cartoons and James Bond—his conclusion being that such phenomena should be analysed as indicative of the society which engendered them.

Eco's first novel was a crafty medieval mystery called *The Name of the Rose*, which quickly became an international best-seller. His subsequent novels, *How to Travel with a Salmon* and *The Island of the Day Before*, are notable for their exuberant narrative and verbal conjuring.

GETTING AROUND

Not so long ago Italy was still cut off from the rest of Europe by the Alps. Napoleon built the Simplon Pass at the beginning of the 19th century; the railway tunnel was opened in 1906. And though a carriage road was made over the Grand St Bernard in 1905, nearly 60 years went by before motorists could reach Italy all year round—except by the coastal road from France, or with the help of snow chains elsewhere.

Yet a magnetic force for travellers it always was. Strabo found Englishmen in Rome during the first century AD. In 1027, King Canute made his way to the Vatican—mainly to seek a reduction of the tolls levied on pilgrims who passed through the papal territories. According to Villani, the Italian historian, 30,000 pilgrims reached Rome on a single day in 1300, the first Holy Year. By 1450, there were more than 40,000 of them, herded into hospices like cattle.

To reach the Eternal City they had endured tremendous hardships, for travelling in the old days was risky and adventurous. Tracks over the Alps were often blotted out by sudden snowstorms or avalanches. In the plains, bands of robbers were on the look-out for visitors, and there was always the danger of getting caught up in a battle or a military operation.

Coming by sea was not much safer. Ships were wrecked by storms, or attacked by pirates who took everyone on board prisoner.

Yet despite all the hazards and discomforts, more people went to Italy than to any other country. Students came to study at the Italian universities, which had the greatest collections of manuscripts before the invention of printing. (Since Latin was the language used by cultured Europeans, they may have found it easier to work in Bologna, Padua or Siena than exchange students do today.) Poets, painters and architects came to learn their arts, doctors, scientists and lawyers to improve their knowledge, merchants to trade.

By the 15th century, Italy had become the richest, most dazzling, most cultured part of Europe. New discoveries and commercial activities had produced unimaginable wealth —stimulating intellectual speculations, a blossoming of art and a refinement of living. From all over the continent people flocked in to see what was happening in Italy, to bask in the brilliance of the Florentine Renaissance.

Despite dire warnings that lust, violence and filth lurked beneath the surface of this glittering social scene, wealthy families sent their sons and sometimes their daughters to enrich their culture at a time when the rest of Europe was still comparatively barbaric.

And so the concept of the 'Grand Tour' came about. By the 18th century, a lengthy visit to Florence, Rome, Naples and Venice had become an indispensable part of any aristocratic education. Dr Johnson declared: 'A man who has not been to

Fountains like this one can still be found in working order.

Italy is always conscious of an inferiority, for his not having seen what it is expected a man to see.' Italy had become a status symbol.

THE GRAND TOUR

Grand tourists were advised to carry a snuff box or a scented handkerchief as a safeguard against unpleasant smells, and to include in their equipment such items as insect powder, foot warmers, money belts, kettles for boiling water and portable lavatory seats—all of which the modern visitor may safely leave at home.

Wealthy and cultured aristocrats came in their hundreds. The British were so numerous that their couriers had trouble hiring horses for the journey; the Piazza di Spagna in Rome was dubbed 'the ghetto of the English'. Shortly before the Battle of Waterloo, a cricket match was held in Naples between Eton and the rest of the world (which the Etonians won by an inning).

Many of these visitors—like the Brownings—were passionate supporters of Italian unity during the last few years of papal secular rule, though being Protestants, they counted for little politically. There was a British minister in

In Rome, you can enjoy a quiet drink at Trastevere in the middle of the day. But at night, the square is a hive of activity.

Florence (the redoubtable Horace Mann) but no diplomatic representative in Rome until after 1870. This did not stop Italians from admiring the English, despite their eccentricities, for possessing a parliament that governed so much of the world, for their country's industrial development—and their own evident wealth.

Quotes from Grand Tourists

- Goethe published his own guide for visitors in 1789. He regarded the Roman carnivals as a throwback to the ancient Saturnalia—streets festooned with floral decorations, tapestries, lights, saloons, galleries and strident crowds. Masks were to be seen everywhere—some mimicking ancient Rome, others the commedia *dell'arte*—along with a host of military uniforms and folk costumes. The Corso was jammed by long lines of decorated carriages; people of all kinds were there to look and be looked at.

  They were entertained by furious battles of confetti, perfumed eggs and candied almonds; by marionette shows, pantomimes and dances in the theatres. Every evening there were parades, horse races and banquets. Goethe thought it was 'one of the most beautiful shows in today's world... not given to the people, but by the people to themselves.'

  The crowded streets, the fancy dresses and the unexpected spectacles struck him as being a metaphor of life itself. 'Freedom and equality can only be enjoyed in the turmoil of folly.' 'Certainly,' he concluded, 'people out of Rome have no idea how one is schooled here. One has to be born again, so to speak, and one learns to look back on one's old ideas as upon the shores of childhood.'

- Stendhal reckoned that the festivities were indicative of the national and regional character of Italians. Florentines had been transformed by their Grand Duke 'into many devout sopranos. They are not interested in anything, by now, but beautiful liveries and pretty processions.' South of the Tiber 'you will find the energy and the joyfulness of savages', while in the Papal States (Lazio, Umbria, Marche and part of Emilia-Romagna) the only law enforced is 'the observance of rituals', and in Naples 'the adoration of St Gennaro'.

The climate alone 'produces a nervous and inexplicable effect on arriving foreigners,' he declared, tossing off a Gallic gem: 'The charm of Italy is akin to that of being in love.'

- Gogol had no doubts. 'Who has been in Italy can forget all other regions,' he wrote euphorically. 'Who has been in heaven does not desire the earth. Europe compared to Italy is like a gloomy day compared to sunshine.'

- But Oscar Wilde, after getting drenched on a gondola trip in Venice, said he felt as if he had 'travelled through sewers in a coffin'.

- The Marquis de Sade was much taken by Zumbo's three small wax compositions in the Bargello representing the plague in Rome, Florence and Milan. 'There one can observe all the different degrees of dissolution, from the fresh cadaver to the one the worms have completely devoured,' noted this connoisseur of the macabre. 'One instinctively takes the hand to the nose. It is hard to consider these horrible images without recalling the sinister ideas of destruction, and consequently the more comforting one of the Creator.'

- Anatole France, contemplating Florence from the Fiesole heights, exclaimed that 'nowhere else is nature so subtle, elegant and fine. The God who made the hills of Florence was an artist.'

- To Aldous Huxley, Tuscany (as seen from the same spot) was 'the kingdom of silence and solemn beauty'. And the colours, 'golden lights and violet shadows floating like the disembodied essence of a landscape'. 'Here at the heart of it,' he thought, 'a man might begin to understand something about that part of his being which does not reveal himself in the quotidian commerce of life; which the social contacts do not draw forth …'

- Louis Kahn, one of the greatest of modern architects, had this to say: 'I've seen in the streets of Florence, on the faces of the people, the happiness of those who still work with their hands, the same of the painters, of the sculptors. You must not lose it. Mankind is losing it, almost everywhere …'. 'It would be enough,' he instances, 'to listen to what in silence says that unique pure space of your Baptistry [of Florence]. In it there is the structure of the future. Very clear!'

Today's Grand Tour

Today, the Grand Tour can be undertaken with a great deal less trouble and in a much shorter time. The problems are not carriages groaning up alpine passes and flea-infested inns, but traffic jams ('We no longer need umbrellas,' laughed a Neapolitan in the middle of a downpour, 'we all have cars') and the sheer pressure of 12 million other tourists who charge into Italy every year, mostly at the same time. This is the biggest culture shock of all.

So the rules have changed. Rather than head for the big cities, it is better for motorists to give them a wide berth. No longer can you sweep into Milan after negotiating the St Gotthard or the Simplon and come to rest in front of the Principe di Aosta or some similar hotel, for the very good reason that it's hardly possible to drive into the city centre, let alone find anywhere to park. (Anyway such five-star caravanserais are now beyond the means of anyone not in the bank-raiding business.)

The same goes for most of the traditional ports of call. In Venice, of course, it has always been necessary to leave cars outside the city—a practice you would be well advised to follow in most other places.

But don't let this put you off. On no account should you miss visiting Florence and Rome, where so many of Italy's great works of art are to be found, or indeed other major cities. But when you embark on your own 'grand tour', do as Italians do—use public transport whenever you can. Fortunately most of these places have airports as well as direct railway connections. The guide books will tell you what to look for, and give all the information you need to know about each city and its sights.

Minor Tours

It is tempting, if you have never been to Italy before, to join a package tour. In that way your itinerary will have been established in advance—hotel reservations made, sightseeing organised, buses laid on, meals organised. You will be shepherded around by a competent guide who will tell you what's what, and sort out any problems that arise. There won't be any hassles, and everything but your personal expenses will be included in the deal. All you have to do is keep to the schedule.

Tempting, yes. The snag is that you become cannon fodder for the travel industries. You will be tied hand to foot. If it rains and the schedule is thrown askew, you will still have to follow it. You won't be able to stop off in a spot that appeals to you, or linger over anything—a prospect, a picture, an incident—that catches your imagination. You will be an anonymous part of a group, whether you like it or not. You will have kissed goodbye to independence.

The solution is to disperse, go underground—set off on your own, without any timetable or a single reservation. Take the car (or hire one), count the days at your disposal, and sally forth on your own four wheels to discover what Italy has to offer.

This way you'll get to know the country better than by looking at the conventional sights, and be able to intuit its true spirit. You'll discover, what's more, that even minor Italian artistry is great art too.

If this isn't practical, at least you can find time to embark on a mini-tour of the surrounding countryside.

From Milan

Milan is the economic capital—even its scandals are carried out in a business-like fashion. From there, have a look at the Italian lakes, starting with Lake Como—you can potter around Bellagio and take a ferry to Punta Ballnanello and then motor over the hills to Lake Garda. Alternatively, head for Stresa on Lake Maggiore, and take a launch to the Borromean Islands.

From Turin

Turin was the capital of the Savoy kings, double-breasted and dignified. You might indulge in a gastronomic jaunt to Alba (truffles), Asti (Spumante), Casale Monferrato (Barolo) and Vercelli (risotto in the old town).

From Venice

This is the gateway to the Orient, and the trick is to take a boat trip along the poplar-lined Brenta Canal—it's the best way to see the splendid Palladian villas between Fusina and Stra. You can look in on Padua too. Another option is to drive up the autostrada and spend a day or two in the Dolomites.

From Genoa

From the biggest seaport in Italy, you'll find it delightful to motor along the twisty Riviera road to Camogli, Portofino and the Cinque Terre. (Until a few years ago, places like Moneglia, Levanto and Portovenere were inaccessible by road.)

There are plenty of beautiful buildings to visit throughout Italy.

From Bologna

Bologna is characterised by *la grassa e la dotta*—food and academe. From here, make an expedition to see the Byzantine mosaics at Ravenna, San Marino (Europe's oldest independent state) as well as Pesaro and Urbino in the Marche.

From Florence

Florence was the capital of Renaissance Italy. Taking the city as your base, you can explore Tuscany. Drive through the vineyards of Chianti to Siena and you'll be moving from the Renaissance back to the Middle Ages. Further south are Montepulciano, Pienza and Montalcino, splendid small Renaissance towns. On the return leg, don't miss San Gimignano with its towers. Then go on to Volterra, and along the coast to Pisa and Lucca.

Siena is a beautiful city, crammed full of history. Every day in the summer, thousands of tourists throng the Campo.

A lesser-known trip is through the Casentino (birthplace of the Medicis) to Arezzo, and back down the Val d'Arno.

From Rome

Rome is the home of the Romans, Popes and the Baroque. Why not visit 'mystic' Umbria—Orvieto, Todi, Assisi, Spoleto, Lake Trasimene? Alternatively drive through Tivoli to L'Aquila and the Gran Sasso, returning via Sulmona (Ovid's town) and the autostrada from Frosinone.

From Naples

From this former capital of the Bourbon kingdom, you can see how the Romans lived at Pompeii and Herculaneum, and how today's jet-setters disport themselves at Amalfi and Positano—not to mention Capri and Ischia.

From Palermo

Palermo is in Sicily and it is possible to catch a glimpse of Magna Grecia at Agrigento, Ragusa and Syracuse. The best trip of all is right round Sicily, if you can spare a week.

From Cagliari

Almost cut off from official history, Cagliari will allow you to enjoy the contrast between the *nuraghi*—prehistoric conical fortresses made of huge dry-stone walls—and the modern constructions of the Costa Smeralda. The best road runs round the island, but it's quite a long drive.

Off the Beaten Track

Nestling against the Sibillini Mountains about 30 miles (48.3 km) inland from the Adriatic coastline lies Sarnano, a medieval hill-town which is also a thermal spa. It is popular with Italians, but few foreigners ever make their way there. So you can imagine the surprise of the locals to see Prince Charles walking round the main square and chatting with passers-by one morning in May 1989.

The Prince of Wales was on a painting tour of the Marche, a part of Italy that many people had never even heard of. From Pesaro (the birthplace of Rossini) he had gone to Urbino to

High up in the Sibillini Mountains you can come across lakes and rivers where Italian families love to picnic.

see the Ducal Palace; and then motored slowly south, visiting Iesi (where Emperor Frederick II was born), Recanati (home of the poet Leopardi), Loreto (religious sanctuary), Cingoli, Camerino and Macerata. After wandering around Sarnano, he had lunch with Italian friends at Monte San Martino, and ended up at Ascoli Piceno, which is one of Italy's best-kept secrets.

Prince Charles's jaunt through the Marche countryside is an example of the sort of itinerary you can choose if you want to get off the beaten track.

PUBLIC TRANSPORT
Travelling by Rail
In such a long mountainous country it often pays to travel by train. Fortunately the railway system is rather good news, being efficient, inexpensive and, in most respects, enjoyable. The only snags are that trains are liable to be overcrowded, especially in summer, and subject to strikes.

On the main lines, trains vary between high-tech expresses and those with old-fashioned carriages which evoke the velvety comfort of 50 years back. On subsidiary lines local trains chug leisurely between country towns, stopping at every village station to offload schoolchildren and farmers' wives with basketfuls of groceries.

The Different Types of Trains

You can distinguish the trains as follows:

- **TEE (Trans-Europe Express)** or so-called Super Rapido. These are top echelon expresses, often restricted to first class, that stop only at places such as Milan, Bologna, Florence, Rome, Naples or Venice. They entail a hefty supplement on top of the normal fare, and usually require advance reservations. The same goes for Eurostar trains, which have first and second class carriages.
- **Rapido**, which swooshes between the main cities with few intermediary stops, and also involves a supplementary payment.
- **Espresso**, which stops at the main towns (no supplement).
- **Diretto**, which stops more frequently and therefore takes longer.
- **Accelerato**, a euphemism for locale, which is delightful if you want to become acquainted with the countryside, but not if you happen to be in a hurry.
- **Intercity** trains are the latest addition. They are local TEE. They provide the best and fastest connection between major cities. Seats are usually reserved.

Every station has notices showing arrivals and departures. Do make sure what type of train it is before you board, because a *diretto* may leave earlier than a *rapido* but arrive considerably later, and an *accelerato* takes all day to complete the journey, with probably a few changes en route.

In the summer, it is as well to make reservations in advance, certainly for couchettes. Tickets can be bought at travel agents' and at the station, but don't leave it until too late—there will invariably be a long and slow-moving queue if you do. As a last resort you can buy your ticket from the conductor, though this will cost more. You can also upgrade your ticket with him if the train turns out to be uncomfortably full.

Concessionary weekly or monthly unlimited travel tickets are available to foreigners, but must be bought before you reach Italy. Consult your travel agent or a CIT office.

The higher grade trains usually have a restaurant or buffet car; on others there may be an ambulating trolley selling sandwich rolls and bottled drinks. Failing this you can usually rely on vendors or bars at intermediary stations. Some stations even have restaurants offering quite good food, some don't.

Beware: trains do not always leave from the *binario* (platform) which is advertised, so check on the spot. There may have been a last-minute change. Moreover certain carriages do not go to the same destination as the rest of the train—make sure you're in the appropriate one. Double-check, too, that your ticket is valid for the day you travel, and that no strike is due to take place anywhere along your itinerary.

Above all, take particular care to safeguard your belongings on overnight journeys so that they don't get rifled while you are asleep.

Incidentally, you can leave your bags on arrival in the station *deposito bagagli* for a few hours, or even days. But ask the staff at what time they knock off—you don't want to find it closed when you're about to leave.

Important: Always remember to 'validate' your ticket by punching it in one of the yellow machines at the entrance to the platform before boarding the train.

By Coach

Buses are an alternative to rail travel, and sometimes quicker, especially in the country. In some areas they are the only form of public transport available.

Buses usually leave from the vicinity of the station, or failing that, the town centre. The destination is indicated on the front, and by the door you will be confronted with an admonitory sign saying (literally) 'Arm yourself with a ticket on the ground and obliterate it on board.' This means that you should buy a ticket—at the nearest tobacconist's or bar —before you get in, and punch it in the machine at the back of the bus. If you can't get hold of a ticket before the bus leaves, the only thing to do is throw yourself at the mercy of the driver; if he's in a good mood he'll probably point to an adjacent shop and wait while you buy it.

Your bags can be stored in the luggage compartment beneath the vehicle.

Buses are somehow more companionable than trains, and you get a better view of the countryside as well as the picturesque villages on the way. You may not be able to lounge in lordly comfort, but at least you can look down on the Bummers and Mercs.

Two-Wheels

Motorbikes and bicycles are difficult to hire and dicey to ride in Italian traffic, unless you're a dab hand. Certainly the twisting hilly roads are no place for beginners. But bicycles can be transported from abroad by rail, and if you happen to be a keen cyclist there's no more down-to-earth way than a bike for getting to grips with some of Europe's most enchanting scenery.

Hiking

Sign-posted trails are few and far between, and, generally speaking, the Italian countryside is not all that suitable for serious hiking. But a number of mountain excursions in the Alps, the Dolomites and the Apennines are organised by the Italian Alpine Club (CAI).

Horse Riding

This is increasingly popular, especially in Tuscany where a number of rent-a-horse stables have mushroomed up. They offer packages including accommodation and riding tours. If you are keen on this type of touring, contact Agriturist or the National Association of Equestrian Tourism (ANTE).

You don't have to go on a horse-riding holiday to meet these friendly creatures. This brief encounter took place high up in the Apennines where horses still roam freely around the uplands.

RECREATION

Your leisure activities will depend on where you are. Along the coast there will be plenty of places to bathe, sail and go fishing.

Tennis courts have sprung up everywhere, and the national sports are football, basketball, as well as cycling.

Golf, until recently an elite recreation, is beginning to catch on, although there are still not many courses. Squash, badminton and croquet are unknown, just as are cricket and baseball.

Up in the Dolomites, the Alps and the Apennines, there are plenty of winter sports resorts.

In the countryside, the passion is for hunting and shooting almost anything that flies—even songbirds—as well as wild boar and hares. Fishing in the rivers and lakes is also a popular pastime; this includes hooking trout that have been bred in artificial lagoons. In places such as the Maremma or Chianti you can rent horses and go on riding tours through the vineyards and woods. You can also join in communal activities, such as playing in the local band. And, in season, help pick the grapes and the olives. Every town and village has its *fiesta* on the local saint's day, with fireworks, roast suckling pig, and dancing in the *piazza*.

An opera house is never far off—there are no less than 27 in the Marche alone. In the summer there are open-air operatic seasons, notably at Verona, Macerata and the Baths of Caracalla in Rome.

Italians like to spend the evening drinking coffee or eating ice cream in the local bar and playing billiards or cards.

On Sunday mornings, many of them still go to Mass (in the countryside the women used to sit in front, while the men stood discussing crops at the back) and after that the whole family goes out for lunch at a restaurant. Between 1:00 pm and 3:00 pm the roads are completely empty—a good time to travel. Though the country is Catholic, non-Catholics are welcome to join in the services. Other denominations will have to go into the cities to find their own places of worship.

Clubs are inclined to be activity centres and thus less socially-oriented than in England or the USA. They tend to focus on a particular pursuit, such as tennis or swimming, and provide facilities for changing along with a coffee bar, but without any clubbiness. Italians, like most Mediterranean people, feel more at home watching TV in a café, or simply passing the time of day by strolling in the *piazza*.

Calendar of Festivals and Holidays

National Holidays	
1 January	New Year's Day
6 January	Epiphany
March/April	Easter Sunday and Monday
25 April	Liberation Day
1 May	Labour Day
2 June	Anniversary of the Republic
15 August	Assumption of the Blessed Virgin Mary
1 November	All Saints' Day
8 December	Immaculate Conception
25 December	Christmas
26 December	Boxing Day

Major Festivals

January	Fair of Sant'Orso in Aosta
February/March	Carnevale in Venice
May	Candle Race in Gubbio
June	Flower Festival in Genzano
July/August	Palio Horserace in Siena
October	Grape Feast in Merano
December	Franciscan Crib in Greccio

Feast Days in Major Cities

25 April	Saint Mark (Venice)
24 June	Saint John (Florence, Genoa, Turin)
29 June	Saints Peter and Paul (Rome)
11 July	Saint Rosalia (Palermo)
19 September	Saint Gennaro (Naples)
4 October	Saint Petronio (Bologna)

LEARNING THE LANGUAGE

CHAPTER 8

'To God I speak Spanish, to women Italian,
to men French, and to my horse—German.'
—Emperor Charles V

CHATTING WITH PEOPLE IS THE BEST WAY to get to know a country and understand its ways. So, whenever you are in a new country, you must first learn the language.

In the case of Italian, anyone who already speaks French or Spanish—these are all Romance languages—will have a definite head start. And if you happen to have studied a few years of Latin at school you will be even further on your way. The reason for this is that contemporary Italian—the language as it is spoken today—is simply the historical and natural evolution of ancient Latin. Nothing more, nothing less.

LATIN

Traces of this continuity can be seen in the idiomatic use of Latin phrases in everyday speech (a characteristic not only of Italian, but of all the Romance languages as well as English). To a great extent, this is due to the influence of the Catholic Church which has continued to use Latin as the official liturgical language. Except at technical establishments, Latin is still taught in Italian schools from the sixth grade upwards.

Remnants of Latin

As a result of the predominance of Latin, a great many Latin tags are still in daily use today. Here are just a few, most of which are well-known enough not to need translating:

- A posteriori–A priori–Ad hoc–Alma mater–Alter ego
- Casus belli–Coitus interruptus–Curriculum vitae
- De facto–De jure–Deus ex machina–Divide e impera
- Ex aequo–Ex libris–Ex novo
- Genius loci
- Habeas corpus–Honoris causa
- In extremis–In vino veritas–Inter nos–Ipso facto
- Lapsus linguae
- Modus vivendi–Mutatis mutandis
- Non plus ultra–Nunc est bibendum
- Pater familias–Per aspera ad astra–Post mortem–Post scriptum–Primus inter pares–Pro capite–Pro loco–Pro memoria–Pro tempore
- Quid pro quo
- Rara avis
- Sine cura–Sine die–Sine qua non–Status quo–Sub judice–Sui generis
- Taedium vitae
- Una tantum
- Vox populi

THE ITALIAN LANGUAGE

After the fall of the Roman Empire, the local variants of the 'vulgar' spoken Latin gave birth to regional dialects. Tuscany being the dominant economic, political and cultural power of the Middle Ages and the Renaissance, the Tuscan dialect came to be adopted as the national language. The works of literary giants such as Dante, Petrarch and Boccaccio —all of whom were Tuscans—set the standards in the 14th century. Dante even wrote a treatise in praise of the new language (though he wrote it in Latin) called *De Vulgari Eloquentia*.

Later, in the 1500s, Bembo and the Accademia della Crusca (which still functions, by the way) codified Tuscan into the official literary and national language. For all this, the regional dialects continued to be used locally in everyday speech, which often caused difficulties. For example, during the Risorgimento—the movement towards national unity in the second half of the 19th century—soldiers were often mystified by orders given by commanders from other regions.

With so many dialects being spoken (and often not fully understood) quite apart from the foreign languages of invaders and visitors, it is not surprising that Italians have always used gestures to make their meaning clear.

BODY LANGUAGE

In any case, 'speaking with their hands'—or all of their bodies in fact!—is in tune with the Italian love of theatrics, and their native gusto for social interaction.

So let's have a look at this body language, which will help you to communicate with Italians:

- When greeting someone, men take their hats off (if they are wearing one), bowing slightly. They may kiss a woman's hand, though this is rather formal. A regular handshake is the normal form of greeting. Close friends of both sexes may hug each other and pat each other's back if they have not met for a long time.
- Patting someone on the shoulder signifies approval: 'Well done!' But flicking the chin outwards with

one's hand means one is not impressed: 'I don't give a damn.'

- Both hands clasped above the head is a sign of triumph: 'I'm the best, we've made it!' A more subtle gesture signifying the same thing is rubbing the fingertips against the lapel of one's jacket: 'Modestly, I'm great!'
- Two fingers held up like a V stands for Victory. But when the index and little finger are outstretched, they represent horns and signify cuckold. Pointed directly at a person, they mean 'bad luck to you'.
- The index finger crossed over the middle finger means the same as in other societies: 'Cross your fingers and hope for the best.'
- Wagging the index finger: 'Watch out. Don't, or else...'
- Fingers crossed in front of the mouth: 'I swear it!'
- Biting one's fingers: 'Damn, I'm mad!' Biting one's lips, on the other hand, means 'Damn, that's bad!'

- Hand raised to the forehead, palm downwards: 'I'm full of it up to here. Sick and tired of it.'
- Drilling one's cheek with a finger: 'Good, delicious.'
- Kissing one's fingers: 'Excellent, deserves a kiss.'
- Moving a hand loosely in front of the body: 'Not again! How boring, what a pain.'
- Hands outstretched, the bottom one beating repeatedly against the top one: 'Go away!'
- Hands outstretched with fingers splayed, moving up and down: 'Take it easy. Calm down. Go slow.'
- Pulling down the bottom eyelid: 'Keep your eyes open! Watch out, he/she is smart.'
- Hand on stomach: 'It's eating me up. I can't stand him/her.'
- Bunched fingers moving up and down: 'What do you want really?'
- Twisting the wrist limply: 'There's not much we can do about it.'
- Hitting a raised arm above the elbow: 'Up yours!' (This is regarded as a particularly rude gesture in Italy.)
- Pulling back both hands with fingers splayed: 'I'll have nothing to do with it.'
- Tapping one's temple: 'You're stupid!' Tapping one's forehead: 'Use your brains!'
- Hand on forehead, little finger outwards: 'Do you think I'm stupid?'
- Thumbing one's nose: 'Marameo!' (Known internationally as the Shanghai gesture.)
- Two hands on forehead: 'Mamma mia! (My God!)'
- Finger moving behind the ear: 'He's a homosexual.'
- Knocking the fist on the table: 'He's really dumb.'
- Tapping a finger against a tooth: 'Not on your life, I won't.'

Touching

Italians touch more than Anglo-Saxons and Asians do. It is usually to show cordiality and goodwill, to communicate. During a conversation an Italian may touch your forearm. This is part of Italian body language and you should not see any meaning in it. Touching the legs, however, while sitting and conversing, indicates intimacy—or the desire for it.

It is common to see two men or two women walking *a fraccetto* (arm in arm). This simply shows friendship. Holding hands, however, means intimacy, as does holding a person around the waist.

In Italy shaking hands is very common. Hugs to bid hello or goodbye are also common, but usually these take place only between old friends. You may also kiss them lightly on both cheeks.

Pinching a woman's buttocks was a common approach a few decades ago, but this behaviour has now disappeared.

LINGUISTIC MINORITIES

When the various feudal states came together in 1860 to form the country we know as Italy, the king of Savoy became the first king of Italy. Like his prime minister Cavour, Victor Emmanuel's first language was French. Consequently he appointed a commission headed by the writer Alessandro Manzoni to propagate the use of Tuscan, the national language.

Tuscan was taught in all the schools. All the same, some minorities continued to cling to their language and culture. About 2.5 million Italians, or 5 per cent of the population, still do so today. These minorities are:

- The German-speaking inhabitants of the Alto Adige and Sud Tirol who became citizens of Italy at the end of World War I.
- The Slavic groups in the provinces of Trieste, Gorizia, Udine, as well as a few in the south around Campobasso.
- Some 95,000 Albanians in the south.
- Gypsies who speak the Sinti dialect in the north, and the Rom dialect in the centre and the south (difficult to say how many there are).
- A small community of Armenians on the island of San Lazzaro in Venice.
- The Langue d'Oc—some 50,000 people who speak provençal in Piedmont, around Turin and Cuneo.

Here are some of the hand gesturses which Italians also use to communicate with.

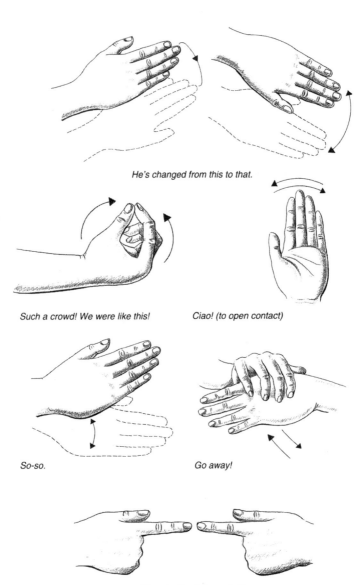

He's changed from this to that.

Such a crowd! We were like this!

Ciao! (to open contact)

So-so.

Go away!

They don't get along at all.

Everything went well.

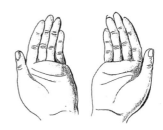

Come over here!

Money, money, money!

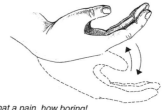

What a pain, how boring!

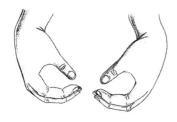

What a big pair of balls! (How boring!)

They really get along!

What a fright!

Watch out!

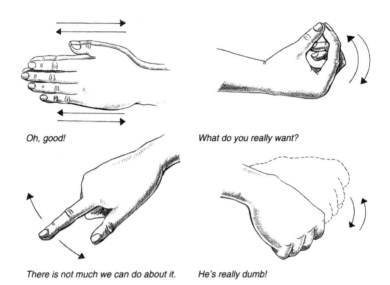

Oh, good!

What do you really want?

There is not much we can do about it.

He's really dumb!

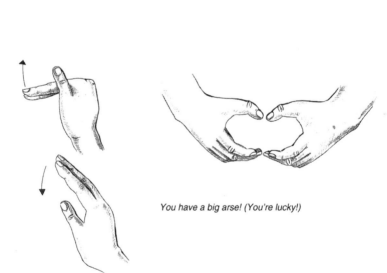

You have a big arse! (You're lucky!)

Bye-bye! (to close contact)

- About three-quarters of the inhabitants of the Valle d'Aosta, who speak a French patois.
- The Catalans in Sardinia who have spoken a language which sounds more French than Spanish since the 14th century.

SPELLING IN ITALIAN

It may happen that you are asked to spell crucial words, and your Italian counterpart does not understand the words you use to spell. Vice versa, your Italian counterpart may spell a word that you don't understand with other words you don't understand either. There is not an Italian standard spelling. Italians use creatively their language, and generally use names of cities while spelling for each other.

Often they will resort to the names of their obscure hometown, or cities in the area, to find examples of words carrying the initials needed. This is not to mention their difficulty with letters such as W, X and Y. So here is the international spelling used in airports and in international organisations. You are better off starting with this, and in due time you may learn the Italian way to spell R as in Rome, D as in Domodossola, P as in Poggibonsi and so on.

A	*Alfa*
B	*Bravo*
C	*Charlie*
D	*Delta*
E	*Echo*
F	*Foxtrot*
G	*Golf*
H	*Hotel*
I	*India*
J	*Juliet*
K	*Kilo*
L	*Lima*
M	*Mike*

N	*November*
O	*Oscar*
P	*Papa*
Q	*Quebec*
R	*Romeo*
S	*Sierra*
T	*Tango*
U	*Uniform*
V	*Victor*
W	*Whiskey*
X	*Xray*
Y	*Yankee*
Z	*Zulu*

If you want an unofficial set of Italian words which are commonly used in spelling, take:

A	*Asti*
B	*Bergamo*
C	*Caltanissetta*
D	*Domodossola*
E	*Enna*
F	*Firenze*
G	*Genova*
H	*Holen (near Bolzano)*
I	*Imperia*
J	*Jesolo (near Venice)*
K	*Kamma (near Trapani)*
L	*L' Aquila*
M	*Macerata*
N	*Napoli*
O	*Otranto*
P	*Padova*
Q	*Quarto (near Naples)*

R	Roma
S	Sondrio
T	Taranto
U	Ustica
V	Venezia
Z	Zagarolo

Italian toponomastic even has W as in Waldbruch (near Bolzano) and X as in Xitta (near Trapani) but you won't find these used at the other end of the peninsula.

WEEDING OUT FOREIGN INFLUENCES

The Fascist regime of the 1930s–1940s tried to pressurise the various ethnic groups into the national culture. At the same time Mussolini waged a linguistic war aimed at eliminating foreign words from Italian.

His campaign to clean up Italian brought some brand new expressions into the language: thus in soccer, goal became *meta* and corner became *angolo*. Mussolini's MINCULPOP (ministry for popular culture) turned Donald Duck into Paperino, Mickey Mouse into Topolino (which was also Fiat's first popular car) and Goofy into Pippo. In jazz, St Louis Blues became *Le tristezze di San Luigi*. But Fascism lost the battle, and these words have now disappeared from the Italian vocabulary. After World War II, the age of Westernisation progressively took over, and now English is the second language of the younger generation of Italians.

ANGLICISMS

Here are some 200 English words that Italians currently use, and which you may also find useful:

- All right–art director–audience
- Baby sitter–background–barbecue–bed & breakfast–bitter–blackout–black tie–blazer–blue chip–blue collar –bluff–body building–box–boyfriend–briefing–broker –brunch–budget–bungalow–buyer–bye bye

- Cafeteria–camera–campus–caravan–cardigan–cash–casual challenge–charter–check–chewing gum–chip–clan–club–cocktail–coffee break–computer–connection–container–copyright–copywriter–corner–countdown
- Dancing–dandy–darling–design–disc jockey–dribbling–drink–drive-in–dry
- Escalation–establishment–executive
- Fashion–fast food–feeling–fiction–fifty-fifty–flash–flirt–franchising–freezer
- Gadget–gag–game–gay–gentleman–girlfriend–glamour–globe-trotter–goodbye–grill–gulp
- Hamburger–handling–happening–hi-fi–hippy–hi-tech–hostess–hot dog–humour
- Impasse–input
- Jazz–jeans–jeep–jelly–jersey–jet–jockey–jukebox–jumbo
- Ketchup–killer–king-size–knock out
- Lady–laser–layout–leader–leasing–limousine–lobby–look–love–lunch
- Mailing–make up–manager–marketing–mass-media–master–match–meeting–merchandising–mix–monitor–musical
- Network–nurse
- Off limits–off shore–okay–old-fashioned–open–optional–out–outdoor–output–outsider–overdose
- Paperback–partner–party–performance–pick-up–picnic–playback–playboy–pocket money–pole position–popcorn–privacy–pub–public relations–Pullman–punch–punk–puzzle
- Quiz
- Racket–raid–recital–record–relax–residence–revival–robot
- Safari–sandwich–scooter–script–self-control–sex appeal–sexy–shock–shampoo–shopping–show–single–sketch–slang–smoking–snack–snob–software–speaker–spider–spoiler–sponsor–spot–spray–sprint–staff– standard–star–starter–station wagon–status–stop–stress–striptease–stylist–supporter–suspense–swing–symbol

- Talk show–target–team–teenager–test–thriller–top–transit–trend–trip–trust–turnover
- Underground–unisex–uppercut
- Vamp–VIP–visa–voucher
- Walkie-talkie–way of life–weekend–western–work in progress
- Yacht–Yankee–yuppie

FALSE FRIENDS

But you should be careful not to rely too much on your English when speaking Italian. Quite a few words seem the same, or very similar, in the two languages—but their meaning is quite different.

- *Bravo*   clever; brave is *coraggioso*
- *Caldo*   hot; cold is *freddo*
- *Camera*   room; a camera is *una macchina fotografica*
- *Cina*   China (the country); China (porcelain) is *porcellane*
- *Confidenza*   familiarity; confidence is *fiducia*
- *Delusione*   disappointment; delusion is *illusione*
- *Disgrazia*   misfortune; disgrace is *disonore*
- *Estate*   summer; estate is *tenuta*
- *Fattoria*   farm; factory is *fabbrica*
- *Gentile*   kind; genteel is *raffinato*
- *Ingenuità*   ingenuousness; ingenuity is *ingegnosità*
- *Lettura*   reading; lecture is *conferenza*
- *Morbido*   soft; morbid is *morboso*
- *Notizia*   news; notice is *avviso*
- *Ostrica*   oyster; ostrich is *struzzo*
- *Parenti*   relatives; parents is *genitori*
- *Recipiente*   receptacle; recipient is *ricevente*
- *Romanzo*   novel; romance is *storia d'amore*
- *Rumore*   noise; rumour is *voce*
- *Scolaro*   schoolboy; scholar is *studioso*
- *Triviale*   vulgar; trivial is *banale*
- *Tutore*   guardian; tutor is *insegnante*
- *Vegetali*   plants; vegetables is *verdura*

Relaxing in a local park is a good way to pick up some of the local dialect.

THE LANGUAGE IN DAILY USE

Nowadays television and the press have imposed a new style of language, mixing the standard Italian of Tuscan origin with the Roman and Milanese speech of the country's political and economic capitals.

Yet despite the trend towards homogenisation, the Italian language remains full of intriguing flavours and colours. Take, for instance, the insults you are likely to hear if you witness one of those proverbial outbursts of Italian temper:

Insults Based on Zoology

Animale	animal
Asino	donkey
Babbeo (or *babbuino*)	baboon
Bestia	beast
Cane	dog
Maiale (or *porco*)	pig
Mostro	monster
Pachiderma	pachyderm
Pidocchio	lice (*pidocchio rifatto* is pretentious lice)
Piattola	bug
Scimmione	big ape
Serpe	snake
Somaro	arse
Verme	worm

Insults Based on Sexual Behaviour

Becco, cornuto	cuckold
Cazzone, minchia	prick
Checca	queen
Coglione	testicle
Culo	arse (*buco di culo* is arse hole)

Degenerato	degenerate
Depravato	depraved
Frocio	homosexual
Mezz'omo	half man
Pappone, mantenuto	pimp
Pervertito	pervert
Puttana, maiala, troia, mignotta, squaldrina	whore
Sporcaccione, zozzone	dirty old man
Testa di cazzo	prickhead

Insults Based on Stupidity

Cretino	cretin
Idiota	idiot
Matto	crazy
Imbecille	imbecile
Pazzo	mad
Rincoglionito, rimbambito, rincitrullito	senile
Stupido, ebete	stupid

Insults Based on Cleanliness and Dirt

Merda, merdoso, pezzo di merda	shit, piece of shit
Pidocchioso	full of lice
Puzzone, fetente	stinker
Stronzo	turd

Insults Based on Social Behaviour

Bandito	bandit
Brigante	brigand
Contadino	peasant

Delinquente, canaglia, mascalzone, farabutto	criminal
Ladro	thief
Menagramo, jettatore, uccello del malaugurio	person of ill omen
Traditore	traitor
Ubriaco	drunkard
Vigliacco	coward
Villano	ill-mannered boor

Insults Based on Family

Figlio di un cane	son of a dog
Figlio di troia	son of a bitch
Mortacci tua	a plague on your ancestors

Endearments

Yet Italians and their language can be very sweet. Here, by contrast, are some colourful terms of endearment:

Amore mio	my love
Angelo	angel
Biscottino	little cookie
Bistecchina	little steak
Caro (masculine), cara (feminine)	dear
Carissimo, carissima	dearest
Dolcezza mia	my sweetness
Fragolina	little strawberry
Gucci-pucci, ebo-lebo	onomatopoeic nonsense
Luce degli occhi miei	light of my eyes
Meraviglioso	marvellous
Meringhina	little pastry
Mia principessa	my princess
Mia regina	my queen

Micio	kitten, *coniglietto* is bunny
Mio principe azzurro	my handsome prince
Tesoro	my treasure
Vita mia	my life, *anima mia* is my soul
Vivo per te	I live for you
Zuccherino	little sugar

LEARNING ITALIAN

It is easy to pick up enough Italian to find your way around or order a meal, but difficult to speak the language correctly and elegantly. In grammar, one often feels, the exceptions come near to proving that there is no rule.

For instance, to say 'you' one can use either the second person singular, the third person singular, the second person plural or the third person plural. Which one you use is according to the degree of intimacy or respect one wishes to convey.

In the Marche (and most advertisements) the personal pronoun *tu* is ubiquitous, but in most other regions this would be regarded as over-familiar outside family circles. So it's safer to address people as *lei*, despite the fact that this literally means 'her', and to go on speaking as if the person were absent. Do not be put out, either, when in letters neither the addresser nor the addressee is mentioned at all, and the message begins without the usual 'Dear Sir' or 'Dear Madam'.

Nor is there cause for concern when an official communication requests you to act *tempestivamente*. This does not solicit a tempestuous reaction, but simply that you do whatever is necessary at the appropriate moment. If you are told to *denunciare* your residence, it does not imply that you should complain about the place you are staying in, but simply give the address. To be *ricoverato all'ospedale* does not signify that you have recovered in hospital, but merely that you have been taken to one. And if the word *concussione* is mentioned, it does not mean that someone has been bashed on the head but the more sinister suggestion that

Buying the morning newspapers in Rome.

he is suspected of extortion. When you've enjoyed a tender steak it is quite acceptable to say that it was *morbida*. But don't express your pleasure by telling the waiter that the meal was very sophisticated or *sofisticato* because this would imply that the food was so adulterated that you ought to lodge a complaint with the health authorities.

Italian Names
Finally, remember that in Italy the family name is usually put first, so that (officially at least) you will be addressed as Smith John or Doolittle Eliza; and that in the eyes of the bureaucracy a woman always retains her maiden name.

'Working enobles man—and makes him similar to the beast'
—Italian proverb

The Romans practised a form of marine insurance known as 'bottomry'—which they probably inherited from the Etruscans—and Plutarch records that Cato the Censor was a great money-lender. In the Middle Ages, the Italians had a near monopoly in banking for, as financiers to the Vatican, they handled the vast taxes levied by Rome.

The Florentines invented the draft bill of exchange; the Sienese developed double-entry bookkeeping; the Medici bank anticipated the holding company of today. It was the 'Pope's merchants' or Lombards—those Italians after whom the famous street in London is named—who introduced banking and insurance to England. Even today the wording of a Lloyd's policy reflects its Italian derivation (*polizza*, a promise or undertaking).

So when you do business in Italy you are dealing with people who have trade in their blood. Some of Europe's greatest industrial combines are in the north, some of the shrewdest minds in the south. To compete with them you have to get up very early in the morning.

SNAGS

The greatest hurdle to be overcome is Italy's all-pervasive, Kafka-esque bureaucracy. That, and the insidious corruption which for decades infected most government departments. The 'Clean Hands' revolution of 1992–1994 was largely directed against such abuses, and there is reason to hope that a new dispensation will be able to cure these ills and rescue the economy. Already there are signs of improvement.

The complications of the tax system are mind-blowing, too. Taxes are disproportionately heavy—President Einaudi once stated that if they were all collected Italians would pay 150 per cent of their incomes! As a result, taxes tend to be paid in the north but less often in the south, where it is estimated that 15 per cent of the population evade them completely. This is a perplexing matter that the authorities are beginning to address seriously.

The legal system is equally chaotic. Thirty years ago a distinguished jurist commented that Italy was the land of '250,000 laws'. Since then the number of laws has more than doubled, and unrepealed acts from Roman times, the Middle Ages, the Bourbon period, the Napoleonic code, the Kingdom of Italy and the Fascist regime still exist side-by-side with modern legislature, allowing plenty of scope for litigation. Often a new law is modified several times after it reaches the statute book, and on top of all this come a stream of EU directives from Brussels. If ordinary people are baffled, so are many lawyers.

STARTING OUT
The new single market means, in theory at least, that the barriers are down and European nationals can operate in other EU countries as freely as they do in their own. But setting up on one's home ground is relatively simple compared to venturing into an unfamiliar environment where the ways of doing business, as well as the culture and the language, are quite different.

Gaps In The Market
Obviously, the first priority is to carry out what is grandly called a feasibility study—or in simple terms, check out the market to make sure your business venture will not flop.

The next priority is to learn the language. This is especially important in Italy where success will depend on being able to communicate with a whole heap of people who probably don't speak your language. (In fairness, why should they?)

The Italian entrepreneur can be found in the company boardroom as well as by the roadside and at open-air markets.

Moreover to become involved in the life of a place you must be fluent in its tongue. That's only common sense.

Opportunities for expatriates to work in Italy are increasing daily, so there is plenty of scope for those who seek employment or contemplate starting up on their own.

There are chances of employment in one of the many Italian or international companies which require specialised skills. Under EU rules, qualified professionals in no less than 92 activities are already accepted by member countries, and the list is likely to embrace further trades and qualifications before long.

What this means is that EU citizens have the right to work in Italy provided they apply for a work permit, and are free to nail up their nameplates if they wish to launch out on their own. These privileges are not, of course, extended to nationals of countries outside the European Union.

Procedures

To operate commercially, you must have a recognised business licence. Self-employed individuals are required to register at the commune where they intend to work. This is relatively simple and fine if you intend to go solo. The trouble is that you will be taxed at source, often excessively.

Rome is the seat of government, the political and administrative capital of Italy.

Simple partnerships can be formed between a minimum of two people, who are obliged to keep a journal and inventory register, as well as invoices of all purchases and copies of business correspondence. Moreover the participants are personally responsible for debts.

Other partnership structures are:

- *Società in nome collettivo* (Snc), a general partnership with unlimited liability
- *Società in accomandita semplice* (Sas): in this case the liability of individual partners is restricted to the capital they have invested
- *Società in accomandita per Azioni* (SapA), a partnership in which the managing partner's liability is unlimited

Company structures are:

- *Società per Azioni* (SpA), the equivalent of a British limited liability company. It has to be incorporated by public deed and have a minimum capital of 10,000 euros (of which 30 per cent must be deposited with the Bank of Italy until the formalities of registration are completed). To be quoted on the stock exchange requires a minimum capital of 100,000 euros.

- *Società a responsibilità limitata* (Srl), a private company financed by individual participants whose liability is limited to their share in it. It is less costly to set up than an SpA and does not require the appointment of an outside auditor if the capital is under 50,000 euros.

Setting up a company, or even a partnership, is complicated and expensive. The golden rule is to appoint an accountancy firm to guide you through the formalities, and to employ an expert *commercialista* (business advisor) to deal with your fiscal affairs.

An alternative option is to acquire an existing concern. This saves time and avoids much of the bureaucratic hassle. On the other hand you must be absolutely sure of what you are taking over, and the obligations you will have to shoulder. A sound balance sheet is not enough—it is essential to take advice from a first-class accountancy firm before making a move.

For instance, relations between employers and staff are controlled by a mass of social and labour legislation, which is noticeably more protective towards employees than in other EU countries. Great care is necessary to prevent you from being saddled with inefficient staff who cannot be dismissed. In short, if the rewards from doing business in Italy are great, so are the hazards.

> If you are tempted to take the plunge, we suggest that you consult the local Italian Chamber of Commerce, as well as the United States Foreign and Commercial Service or one of the British Chambers of Commerce in Italy. These bodies, like the commercial section of the Italian Embassy, will be able to tell you, if you are not an EU citizen, how to set about establishing yourself in Italy.

BUSINESS ETIQUETTE

The pleasant aspect, of course, is that Italians are warm, outgoing people with whom doing business is enjoyable, even fun. Negotiations are conducted in a leisurely fashion, often over a protracted and convivial lunch. It is an asset to know something about the regional specialities that are being offered (*see Food And Entertaining chapter*) and to be able to hold your own on such topics as literature and art.

But friendly and relaxed though the atmosphere may be, you'll find that business procedures are more old-fashioned and status conscious than in many other places. The company hierarchy is carefully observed and top executives don't usually muck in with the lads at the canteen. They may be on first name terms with each other, but at business conferences they are addressed by the titles printed on their visiting cards.

Business Tips

- If you are doing business in Italy, remember that the person making the deal is traditionally as important as the deal itself. The means justify the end. Presence, a positive personable attitude and a follow-up note or greetings for the holiday season will make your counterpart happy to have made a deal with you and ready to consider the next.

- Firmness is respected but the impression of aggressiveness is not. Put a velvet glove over your iron fist if you have one.

- Remember the old adage *'I migliori affari si fanno in due'* (The best deals are the ones that both partners make at the same time.)—not at the expense of the other. Show that you are putting yourself in the other person's position, and understand well his point of view on the deal.

- Traditionally, a word of honour and a handshake were as binding as a contract. It isn't done anymore, but most Italians still romanticise over this old custom. So if the verbal agreements are translated without surprises in a written contract, you may underline them, and even reap some benefits in the next deal.

Initially at least you would do well to follow this practice, which actually simplifies protocol a lot. You won't go far wrong by addressing the boss as *Padrone*, or *Commendatore* if he bears that title, and the others as *Ingegnere* (if technical), *Ragioniere* (financial), *Avvocato* (legal), *Architetto* (architect), *Geometra* (surveyor) and so on, or by the blanket title of *Dottore* (or *Dottoressa*). *Signor* and *Signora* are also acceptable. The dress code also tends to be fairly formal, except on the shop floor.

WORKING HOURS

The normal working week is five days, 40 hours, though shops open on Saturdays and a few private offices do so on Saturday mornings. Business hours vary from the traditional 9:00 am to 1:00 pm and 3:00 pm to 7:00 pm, to the industrial 9:00 am to 5:00 pm followed by most factories and institutions, with an hour's break for lunch. Shops usually open from 9:00 am to 1:00 pm and 5:00 pm to 8:00 pm (or 4.30 pm to 7.30 pm in winter). Some lawyers and other professionals work even later.

Virtually the whole country closes down from 20 July to 20 August, except for the leisure industry for whom the summer holiday break is the peak period of activity. Every employee is entitled to five or six weeks' annual holiday, as well as the statutory national holidays, which are as follows:

- 1 January — New Year's Day (Capodanno)
- 6 January — Epiphany (La Befana)
- March/April — Easter (Pasqua)
- 25 April — Liberation Day
- 1 May — Labour Day (Primo Maggio)
- 15 August — Assumption (Ferragosto)
- 1 November — All Saints' Day (Ognissanti)
- 8 December — Immaculate Conception (L'Immacolata Concezione)
- 25 December — Christmas Day (Natale)
- 26 December — Boxing Day (Santo Stefano)

NEGOTIATIONS

Time is not necessarily money in Italy, and the high pressure approach is not generally appreciated. A few minutes of pleasant conversation enable everyone to become acquainted, after which it should be made clear whether you are fact-finding or have a definite deal in mind.

Italians are subtle negotiators; they prefer shades of grey to stark black and white, so waltz round the subject diplomatically. On the other hand, too much dithering about in the hope of gaining last-minute concessions may have the opposite effect.

ITALIAN FLAIR

Italians possess an innate sense of form and design. They have a genius for pulling something out of the hat. For instance, a village builder will sketch out your fireplace or staircase on the back of an envelope, or a mechanic will improvise some engineering device that would take weeks to work out on the drawing board. Below are two examples of the Italian business genius in action:

The Stylist

Pinin Farina developed car styling into an art, and by the 1950s a number of independent coach-builders had opened ateliers in Turin. Ghia, Vignale, Bertone, Allemani, Fissore all learnt their skills from Farina. They thrived by building special bodies on conventional chassis, many of which were covertly ordered by the big motor manufacturers to inspire their own styling departments.

Yet nearly all these Turin *carrozzerias* used the same freelance stylist. On average some 300 different models were designed for them every year by Giovanni Michelotti.

When Michelotti's name finally appeared on a futuristic British mini-car—the Meadows Frisky—at the Geneva Show in 1957, the diminutive maestro found himself instantly famous.

He was engaged as a consultant by Standard-Triumph who had discovered that prototypes could be made in Turin very quickly and at a fraction of what they would cost in England. Michelotti was told to style a new utility car. He followed the factory's instructions carefully, and the design was approved by the board. But the chief engineer had a hunch that Michelotti could do better if allowed a free hand. How did he think the car should look?

While he was talking Michelotti sketched in the headlights and then, with a slightly curved French ruler, drew a line from beneath them to the rear. His 'dart' line, he called it, and on the spot he developed the theme.

When the chief engineer returned to Michelotti's studio the following morning, he found three tenth-scale coloured pictures along with full-scale coach-builder's drawings of this dart car pinned up on the wall. For a quarter of an hour he studied them without uttering a word.

Finally he drew his breath and said, 'I'll probably lose my job. But forget the board's decision. This is the car we must make.' Thus the Triumph Herald came into being. It turned out to be the company's most successful model, and remained in production for 20 years.

Subsequently Michelotti took some designs for a new Triumph TR4 to the factory, but they weren't what the people

Shopping during your lunchtime is always tempting especially along avenues such as this, Via Borgognona, which harbours many of Rome's designer shops for clothes, shoes, leather goods and other accessories.

at Coventry wanted. (The car's image had been changed —from rugged Anglican male into a luscious Italian female.) 'If I understand correctly,' he commented on the way back to London, 'they want me to design them an ugly car—*una macchina brutta?*'

So overnight at Henley he got busy. His modified version was chunky and aggressive, with hard body lines and hooded headlights flanking the characteristic Triumph grille. It was plug-ugly, but appealing.

When he produced the drawings in London the following afternoon, the chairman of Triumph could hardly believe his eyes. It was just what they wanted. And in due course the TR4 appeared—almost exactly as Michelotti had dreamt it up at the Red Lion in Henley. Now it is regarded as a classic.

Most factories employed squads of stylists who spent months working on a new model. But in a matter of hours Michelotti produced a couple of best-sellers.

Soon, thanks to Pinin Farina and Giorgetto Giugiaro, Turin became the world centre of car design—a striking example of collective individual flair.

The Entrepreneurial Spirit

The Marche, as its plural name suggests, is not one homogeneous region, but a cornucopia of small independent towns—each a little world with its own sense of humour, its distinctive tone of speech, its traditions and its strong sense of identity.

This insular mentality is a common denominator which lies behind its recent industrial development and the success of small family businesses—the 'Marche miracle' which fascinates economists and socialists alike. For how can an agricultural region, where 60 per cent of the population worked in the fields until a few years ago, suddenly become a prime industrial area?

Perhaps the secret lies in the fact that the Marchigiano was always more than a farmer. He had to be an all-rounder —a carpenter, a basket maker, a forester, a mechanic —and his womenfolk worked their own looms. His position as a sharecropper allowed him more responsibility

than a normal farm worker, for his relationship with the landowner (often a smallholder who had a shop or some professional activity in the town) was that of an associate rather than a paid dependant. In other words, he was an embryonic entrepreneur.

Behind the multifarious factories down on the coast lurks a countryman's ethos. Many of the new industrialists may have had some workshop experience before striking out on their own. Few are second-generation businessmen.

Even the larger enterprises are run like old-fashioned British family businesses. In a typical case the factory will be owned by four or five brothers who have 10 sons between them. Yet before any of these are allowed into the business certain basic principles are laid down.

First, the factory's interests have priority over any personal considerations. Secondly, no interference from wives or outside relatives will be tolerated. Thirdly, no one must draw on the firm's funds for personal requirements. (Dividends, yes. But the capital must remain intact.)

Having accepted these principles the youngsters go through the mill, starting at the bottom. They are encouraged to get together with their siblings and cousins to achieve a communal approach. After four years of apprenticeship each of them is appraised by the managers under whom he has worked—not only for his capabilities, but his personal behaviour. Only then, if he passes muster, will he be admitted to the boardroom.

This strict, almost Victorian initiation gives an insight into the special qualities which distinguish the Marche firms from those in other parts of Italy. Giorgio Fua, the economist, believes their strength lies in the fact that most of them are small and intimately linked to a family. This motivates them to save money rather than spend it, to keep up to date; and provides unusual flexibility to adapt to market conditions. In a period of multinationals, Fua insists that 'small is good'. Today there is one firm to every 100 inhabitants in the Marche, and most of them are guided by a similar work ethic.

SUMMING UP
Italy has some of the world's best business people and some of the world's worst red tape. It is not a place for the faint-hearted or anyone who suffers from high blood pressure.

On the other hand it is a pleasant place to work in and there are countless opportunities for all sorts of activities —such as private care doctors, dentists, nurses, lawyers specialised in international law, veterinarians, plumbers, electricians, mechanics, builders, cabinet-makers, language teachers, real estate agents, marketing experts, farmers—to name but a few.

Small towns offer a pleasant environment
in which to settle and work.

Go solo if you wish; better still team up with a local Italian, because you'll need a friendly hand from someone who has long experience of the country and knows how to deal with the local authorities. This will certainly be the best policy for anyone coming from outside the European Union.

And above all, get yourself a good *commercialista*, and also a clever lawyer!

'Everything happens thanks to ideas; ideas produce facts.'
—Chateaubriand

Capital
Rome

Currency
Euro (EUR)

note: on 1 January 1999, the European Monetary Union introduced the euro as a common currency to be used by financial institutions of member countries; on 1 January 2002, the euro became the sole currency for everyday transactions within the member countries

Government Type
Republic

Administrative Divisions
16 regions (regioni, singular - regione) and four autonomous regions* (regioni autonome, singular - regione autonoma): Abruzzo, Basilicata, Calabria, Campania, Emilia-Romagna, Friuli-Venezia Giulia*, Lazio, Liguria, Lombardia, Marche, Molise, Piemonte, Puglia, Sardegna*, Sicilia, Toscana, Trentino-Alto Adige*, Umbria, Valle d'Aosta* and Veneto

Independence
17 March 1861 (Kingdom of Italy proclaimed; Italy was not finally unified until 1870.)

Climate
Predominantly Mediterranean. Alpine in far north; hot, dry in south.

Area
total: 301,230 sq km (116,305.6 sq miles)
land: 294,020 sq km (113,521.8 sq miles)
water: 7,210 sq km (2,783.8 sq miles)
note: includes Sardinia and Sicily

Agricultural Products
Fruits, vegetables, grapes, potatoes, sugar beets, soybeans, grain, olives; beef, dairy products; fish

Natural Resources
Coal, mercury, zinc, potash, marble, barite, asbestos, pumice, fluorospar, feldspar, pyrite (sulfur), natural gas and crude oil reserves, fish, arable land

Ethnic Groups
Italian (includes small clusters of German-, French- and Slovene-Italians in the north, and Albanian-Italians and Greek-Italians in the south)

Export Commodities
Engineering products, textiles and clothing, production machinery, motor vehicles, transport equipment, chemicals; food, beverages and tobacco; minerals and non-ferrous metals

Gross Domestic Product (GDP)
US$ 1.609 trillion (2004 est.)

Highest Point
Mont Blanc (Monte Bianco) de Courmayeur (4,748 m/ 15,577.4 ft), a secondary peak of Mont Blanc

Lowest Point
Mediterranean Sea: 0 m

Import Commodities
Engineering products, chemicals, transport equipment, energy products, minerals and nonferrous metals, textiles and clothing; food, beverages and tobacco

Internet Country Code
.it

Language
Italian (official), German (parts of Trentino-Alto Adige region are predominantly German-speaking), French (small French-speaking minority in Valle d'Aosta region), Slovene (Slovene-speaking minority in the Trieste-Gorizia area)

Life Expectancy at Birth
total population: 79.68 years
male: 76.75 years
female: 82.81 years (2005 est.)

Literacy
definition: age 15 and over can read and write
total population: 98.6 per cent
male: 99 per cent
female: 98.3 per cent (2003 est.)

Population
total: 57,888,245 (2003)
total: 58,103,033 (July 2005 est.)
average age: 42.3 years (2003)

Religion
Predominantly Roman Catholic with mature Protestant and Jewish communities and a growing Muslim immigrant community

Unemployment Rate
8.7 per cent (2003)

ACRONYMS & ABBREVIATIONS
Government and Business

IVA	*Imposta Valore Aggiunto* (Sales, Tax, Value Added Tax)
SPA	*Società Per Azioni* (Ltd. Inc.)
SR	*Società a Responsabilità* (limited liability)
UE	*Unione Europea* (European Union)
VVUU	*Vigili Urbani* (city police)

Time

AA	*Anno Accademico* (Academic Year)
AC	*Avanti Cristo* (Before Christ)
CA	*Corrente Anno* (of this year)
CM	*Corrente Mese* (of this month)
Sec	*Secolo* (century)

Titles

Cav	*Cavaliere* (Knight)
Comm	*Commendatore* (Commander)
Dr, Dr.ssa	*Dottor, Dottoressa* (Doctor)
On	*Onorevole* (Honourable)
Prof, Prof.ssa	*Professore, Professoressa* (Professor)
SS	*Sua Santità* (His Holiness)
Sen	*Senatore* (Senator)
Sig, Sig.ra	*Signor* (Mr), *Signora* (Mrs)
Sig.na	*Signorina* (Miss and lately Ms)
Ecc.	*Eccellenza (Your Excellency)*

Transportation and Communication

FFSS	*Ferrovie dello Stato* (Italian State Railway)
FNSI	*Federazione Nazionale Stampa Italiana* (Italian National Press Organisation)

CULTURE QUIZ

SITUATION 1

When in Rome you unexpectedly come across an Italian friend you knew at home. He suggests you have dinner together. He picks the restaurant and orders for you because you're not acquainted with the local dishes.

The bill comes and is placed on the table half-way between the two of you. Your friend continues talking and makes no effort to pick it up. You want to leave. You:

A Pay the bill?

B Look at your watch, get up saying 'Thank you for the nice dinner', and leave?

C Pay for the items you have consumed?

D Say *facciamo alla romana* (let's go Dutch) and pay 50 per cent of the bill?

Comments

Answer **D** is correct, because had your friend intended to invite you to dinner he would have made it clear that he was the host, or would have signalled to the waiter to give him the bill. Going Dutch in Italy means splitting the bill in equal parts —itemising would be considered stingy.

SITUATION 2

You're a young male executive on a new job in Italy. Four other people are working in your department. One of them is a sexy young woman in a red miniskirt, who according to office gossip, is wild and unattached.

You suspect she's making overtures to you and are interested in getting to know her. You:

Ⓐ Comment on how sexy Italian women are?

Ⓑ Tell her how sexy she is?

Ⓒ Compliment her effusively on her dress and hairstyle?

Ⓓ Comment on how good she is at her work?

Ⓔ Ask her out for coffee or an aperitif after work?

Comments

Answer ❺ is correct. Flattering comments are not acceptable in the office. You may have misunderstood her behaviour; perhaps she's simply a friendly soul. Her attire may have given you the wrong idea. The situation can be clarified on neutral ground.

SITUATION 3

You have accepted an invitation to visit an Italian family at 5:00 pm. At seven o'clock the conversation is still going strong and you are asked if you'd like to stay for dinner. You happen to be free that evening.

You say:

❶ 'Yes thank you' and stay?

❷ 'Yes, but only if I can help prepare the dinner'?

❸ 'Yes, but only if I can invite you out tomorrow'?

❹ 'Yes, but only if you promise to be my guest when you come to my country?

❺ 'Thank you, but it's impossible tonight. Let's get together before I leave'?

Comments

E is the correct answer. Had they really wanted you for dinner they would have told you ahead of time and not on the spur of the moment. The least they would have done to justify not having invited you properly is to say something like 'We were supposed to be out tonight, but our engagement was cancelled while you were on your way here. So would you join us, please?'

SITUATION 4

The police stop you at a road block at night. You've left your passport at the hotel and are driving a rented car. They say they will have to take you to the police station for checking. You:

A Call it an infringement of human rights and personal freedom?

B Protest and say you want to speak to your consulate before going to the police station?

C Give them your name and nationality and explain where the passport is, asking them to call the hotel and double-check, or offer to go and get it?

D Control your feelings and go to the police station?

Comments

The correct answer is **C**. Very likely they will check and let you go. The police are usually very courteous and understanding with foreigners. But you must realise that under Italian law every citizen—and every foreigner too—is required to produce a proof of identity at all times if asked to do so by the police.

SITUATION 5

You come back to Italy and stop at your favourite grocery store in the local village. The owner wants to bring you up-to-date with everything that has happened in the village since you left. But you are in a hurry. You:

A Walk out saying you'll be back?

B Start helping yourself and put the goods on the counter?

C Apologise for being in a hurry and promise you'll return to catch up with the village news?

D Resign yourself to having to suffer a delay?

Comments

The correct answer is **C**. Personal relationships are very important in Italy. You don't want to give the impression of not caring about the life of the community.

So politely insist on having the shopping done quickly, and allow yourself sufficient time on your next visit to enquire about the local people and goings-on.

SITUATION 6

You are conducting a business meeting, attended by a dozen or more delegates. Things begin to get out of hand—with several people talking at the same time, arguing, interrupting, even quarrelling, and none of them following the agenda. You:

A Stand up and leave?

B Tell yourself that 'while in Rome do as the Italians do' and put up with it?

C Rap the table and make it clear that the meeting must be conducted your way or else proceedings will stop?

ⓓ Reprimand the undisciplined people?

ⓔ Ask the undisciplined ones to leave?

ⓕ Stop the meeting to explain that this is an inter-cultural situation and re-state the rules under which it will be conducted?

Comments

Answer **ⓕ** is correct. Your duty was to define the rules and procedures of the meeting before it began. So apologise first, then lay down the guidelines and make sure that these are followed in the common interest.

SITUATION 7

You are renovating your Italian home. The workers say that they are not accustomed to give written estimates. So you agree to let them redo your roof for approximately 10 million lire. You leave to return a month later to find that the roof has been done in a way you consider unacceptable and the bill is 20 million lire. You:

ⓐ Pay?
ⓑ Bargain?
ⓒ Go to a lawyer?
ⓓ Insist on an itemised bill, then try to get it reduced?

Comments

The answer is **ⓓ**. It's your fault. You should have insisted on having a precise, itemised estimate—which more and more Italian firms are prepared to offer. All you can now do is get an itemised bill, have it checked by the geometra or a reputable firm and the work surveyed. If there are discrepancies, then bargain like mad. Only if the price is still nothing like a fair one should you take the matter to court. (When you calculate the legal fees you may find that it is not worth your while.)

SITUATION 8

I HAVE TO CALL TOKYO, DURBAN AND NEW YORK BEFORE THE FAMILY GETS BACK

You are staying as a house guest with friends. Your hostess tells you to make yourself at home and to help yourself to food or use the phone if you need it. While they are away, you put through several calls to Singapore and New York during the low-rate hours. Upon their return, you:

Ⓐ Say you used the phone as they told you to?

Ⓑ Insist on leaving an appropriate sum of money for the calls?

Ⓒ Ask them to let you know how much you owe them when the bill comes?

Ⓓ Give them a gift 'for the phone'?

Comments

The answer is **Ⓑ**. Italian phone bills are not usually itemised, and your hosts will never know how much you spent. You should have called collect or from a public phone. 'Use the phone' normally means local calls, not inter-continental connections. You are only justified in making a long-distance call if it is a single emergency.

DO'S AND DON'TS

Italians are usually very understanding with foreigners who do not know, but respect and show interest in Italian customs and manners.

The golden rule is to ask politely and apologise smilingly. Let your Italian counterparts know how you would behave in a similar situation in your own culture (without implying yours is better than theirs). Here are some do's and don'ts when interacting with Italians:

DO

- Inform your host early of food taboos and dietary restrictions, if you are invited to a party. (An allergy is always a good excuse, and never questioned!)
- Sit up straight when eating. Keep your elbows close to your body and your forearms on the table.
- Bring your food to your mouth (not your head to your food) and take small bites. Use your napkin only for your lips and always wipe your lips before drinking.
- Answer "*grazie altrettanto*" ("same to you") when your host or hostess says "*Buon appetito*" ("Bon appetit").
- Comment on the food and wine, and compliment the provider.
- Greet others "*buongiorno*" ("good morning") or "*buonasera*" ("good evening"; also "good afternoon"). Make eye contact and smile. The more important person initiates the handshake; the other responds with a firm (not crushing) squeeze.
- Introduce the younger or less important person to the older or more important one.
- Thank the host and hostess, if it is a formal invitation, with flowers and a thank-you note bearing the words "*Grazie per la magnifica serata*" ("Thank you for the wonderful evening")—or a bottle of wine of quality adequate for the occasion with the words "*Per la vostra cantina*" ("For your cellar").

- Print different versions of your name card perhaps some with just your name) to use when you don't need, or don't want, to flash your titles around.
- Ask the older or more important person where they prefer to sit in the car or taxi. Help them to their seat, then go to yours, without asking anyone to move or to open or close a door.
- Wait outside the car (not at the wheel) when picking someone up. When dropping someone off, get out of the car to say goodbye or apologise if the traffic does not allow that.
- Keep your bus ticket handy for inspection or obliteration.
- Offer your seat to passengers who are older, pregnant, disabled, or with children. But do not insist if they refuse your offer, and do not scold other seated passengers for not giving up their seats.
- Turn off your mobile phone at shows, meetings, ceremonies, in sacred places, or where your conversation would infringe on other people's privacy.
  When making a call, ask if it is timely and if the person is a few blocks away or in the South Seas (in which case, he may be paying to receive your call).

DON'T

- Talk with your mouth full or open your mouth when chewing. If anyone asks you anything while you are chewing, swallow before answering.
- Stretch too far for food and drink. Instead, ask "*mi passa l'acqua per favore?*" ("Would you please pass the water?")
- Start eating until everyone has been served and until the hostess starts.
- Clean your plate with bread, not even with your fork, as delicious as the sauce may taste.
- Squeeze someone hard or smooch or pat them on the shoulder when greeting.
- Give red roses to a lady unless you are both intimate.
- Put your name card on your thank-you gift if you bring it to a party you have been invited to.

- Be verbose in congratulations or condolences. Use formulas like *"Congratulazioni vivissime per la tua laurea"* ("Warmest congratulations on your graduation"), *"Auguri e felicitazioni per il nuovo nato/la nuova nata"* ("Best wishes and congratulations for the newborn baby boy/baby girl"), or *"Le più sentite condoglianze per il lutto che vi colpisce"* ("The most heartfelt condolences for the mourning that has struck you").
- Unwrap a gift immediately in a social situation or comment that the gift suits your taste or that you do not already have one like it.

Don't Say

- "I always take your side when I hear gossip about you."
- "Carlo, is this your fiancée? Or just a friend?"
- "Who was the blonde lady in your husband's car last night?"
- "This hat looks nicer than the one you wore at your wedding."
- "Why didn't Dr Rossi invite you to his party last month?"
- "Tell us that wonderful story you always tell!"
- "I know we've met before, but I don't remember your name" or "Are you Mario or Alessandro?"
- "Please come for lunch on Friday. Otherwise, there will be 13 people at the table, and that would be bad luck."
- "With your new hair colour, you look 20 years younger."
- "Is this your granddaughter? Or your daughter?"
- "You look so young in your picture!"
- "I hear you lost your lawsuit. Oh well, you'll win next time."
- "I hear you had an accident. That's nothing compared to what happened to me!"
- "Did you hear we won first prize in the tournament? How did you do?"

Many towns in Italy offer
breathtaking scenery.

GLOSSARY

SIGNS
Accommodation

To Let	*Affittasi*
No Vacancy	*Completo*
Hotel/Inn	*Albergo/Osteria*
Apartment/Flat	*Appartamento*

At the Airport

Arrivals/Departures	*Arrivi/Partenze*
Luggage	*Deposito bagagli*
Customs	*Dogana*

At the Bank

Bank/Savings Bank	*Banca/Cassa di risparmio*
Exchange	*Cambio*

In Shops and Restaurants

Open/Closed	*Aperto/Chiuso*
Information	*Informazioni*
Toilet	*Toilette* (also *bagno, ritirata*)
Reserved	*Riservato*
No Smoking	*Vietato fumare*
Don't Touch	*Vietato toccare*
Family Food Restaurant	*Trattoria*
Inn/Eating place	*Osteria*

On/above Doors

Vacant/Occupied	*Libero/Occupato*
Entrance/Exit	*Entrata/Uscita*

Emergency Exit	*Uscita di sicurezza*
Push/Pull	*Spingere/Tirare*

On Fences

Beware of the Dog	*Attenti al cane*
Keep Out	*Divieto di accesso*
No Swimming	*Divieto di balneazione*
Absolutely No Trespassing	*Limite invalicabile*
Private Property	*Proprietà privata*

On the Road

Stop/Slow Down	*Alt/Rallentare*
Ring Road	*Circonvallazione*
Emergency Parking Zone	*Corsia di emergenza*
Detour	*Deviazione*
No Parking	*Divieto di sosta*
Bus Stop (regular)	
Road Works Ahead	*Lavori in corso*
Underground	*Metropolitana*
Railway Crossing	*Passagio a livello*
Danger	*Pericolo*
One Way	*Senso unico*
Pedestrian Zone	*Zona pedonale*

Products and Services

Sporting goods and equipment	*Articoli sportivi*
Shoe shop	*Calzature*
General shop	*Emporio*
Pharmacy/Chemist	*Farmacia*
Photography	*Fotografia*
Ice cream parlour	*Gelateria*
Jewellery	*Gioielleria*
Book shop	*Libreria*

Optician	*Ottica*
Sandwich/Coffee shop	*Paninoteca*
Hairdresser	*Parrucchiere* (*barbiere* is barber)
Restaurant	*Ristorante*
Smokers' supplies/ postage stamps	*Tabacchi*
Newstand	*Edicola*

RESOURCE GUIDE

Before leaving for Italy, visit these Internet websites: **http://www.altavista.it, http://www.arianna.it, http://www.virgilio.it** and **http://www.yahoo.it**. Generally useful is **http://guide.supereva.it**. While in Italy, use the Yellow Pages to find your way around. Simply call 892-424 and ask for an English-speaking operator, or visit **http://www.paginegialle.it.** The Yellow Pages is also largely available in print.

We thank Dr Alessandro Corsi and Gianluca Marzucchi, who were consulted for the addresses in this brief guide.

EMERGENCY & HEALTH
Emergency Numbers
- **Polizia** (Police)   113
- **Carabinieri** (Carabineers Police)   112
- **Fire Department**   115
- **Health Emergency**   118

All these numbers are toll-free and apply nationwide.

Hospitals
Phone numbers vary from province to province. Find them in the white pages of the local phone book, under *Azienda Ospedaliera. Clinica e Clinica Veterinaria* lists private clinics and animal hospitals.

Medical Services
Look under Medici in the phone book for general practitioners (*medici generici*) and specialists (*specialisti*) in your area. Or visit **http://www.ospedale.net** for a list of public and private hospitals and **http://www.sanita.it**, the health ministry's website.

Dental Clinics
Many hospitals have a dental clinic called a *Clinica Odontoiatrica*. Most Italians, however, go to private dentists. Find these in the phone book under *Dentisti and Odontoiatri.*

LOST AND FOUND SERVICES

Most cities have a *Ufficio Oggetti Smarriti* (lost and found office) operating under the financial branch of services of every municipality. Other reference points are the city police and train stations. If you lose your ID, passport, documents, or anything valuable, you must file a statement with the police.

FACILITIES FOR THE DISABLED

Services and assistance for the disabled are provided by volunteer organisations and the Assessorato Sanità e Servizi Sociali, a branch of the local administration, run by an *Assessore* adjoint to the mayor. The government runs a Ministero degli Affari Sociali e Solidarietà Sociale (Ministry for Social Affairs and Social Solidarity).

HOME & FAMILY
Accommodation
Real Estate Agents

(Agenzie Immobiliari): Most have housing to be rented by the month or week. Visit websites such as **http://www.ecasa.it** for information and offers from the world of real estate.

Rent

Agriturismo and self-catering residences—rooms or apartments for short-term rent in small towns, farms, country homes, or wine estates—are fashionable. Most offer bed and breakfast and local food and wine tasting, usually for a small fee. Check transportation (hotel vans, public buses, cost of taxis to the nearest city or airport).

Hotels

Standards vary by the number of stars earned during periodic checks by public employees of the *Provincia. Lusso* (luxury) is above scale. Two- and one-star hotels are called *Albergo* (hotel), *Pensione* (family hotel) or *Locanda* (country inn). Names can be misleading, so check the facilities and prices in the phone book.

Look for budget hotels in the Yellow Pages and specialised guidebooks. *Ostelli della Gioventù* (youth hostels) are usually good. Some *Casa del Pellegrino* (house of pilgrims) and Catholic convents and monasteries welcome pilgrims and tourists in very suggestive and simple places. Make sure you agree with the atmosphere, rules, and hours (including possible curfews) of the house. *Locande* and *Pensioni* may give special rates for week- and month-long stays. *Affittacamere* and *camere ammobiliate* (rooms for rent, furnished rooms) offer the most inexpensive accommodations.

Childcare

Check the Yellow Pages for babysitters and *nidi d'infanzia* (nursery schools). The latter may be public or private and may take children for a short term. Make sure you agree on times, diet, activities, surveillance (usually very caring) and discipline (usually very lenient), as well as communication between teacher and child.

Schools

Mandatory public schooling consists of five years at *elementari* (elementary) level, three years at *medie* (intermediate) level, and four or five years at *medie superiori* (secondary and high school) level. At the *medie superiori* level, *Liceo Classico* is based on humanistic disciplines, *Liceo Scientifico* on mathematics and sciences, and *Liceo Linguistico* on modern languages. *Istituto Tecnico Commerciale* offers a diploma of *Ragioniere* (accountant), *Istituto Tecnico Agrario* a diploma of *Perito Agrario* (land surveyor), and *Istituto Tecnico per Geometri* a diploma of *Geometra* (building surveyor).

All schools depend on the Ministero per la Pubblica Istruzione (Ministry for Public Instruction); the universities on the Ministero per l'Università (Ministry for the University). Visit **http://www.it-e-loft.com** for information on studying abroad, scholarships, and opportunities. An online magazine for university students is **http://www.campusweb.it**. For sale and exchange of books, notes, and course outlines, most Italian students use

http://www.bakeka.web.com.

Housekeeping
Maids

Some *Agenzie di Lavoro temporaneo* (temporary aid agencies) offer maid services. Or else go to the state *Ufficio del Lavoro* (labour office) of your province. Maids are traditionally found by word of mouth and often become part of the family. Check with your *commercialista* for details of contracts, hourly salaries, and laws (national and local) governing the world of *collaboratrici familiari* (family collaborators).

Laundromats

Find these in the Yellow Pages under *Lavanderie* self-service and *acqua e a secco* (self-service laundry and dry cleaning).

Other Services

Check with the owners; they usually have someone servicing their home. Otherwise, *elettricisti* (electricians), *idraulici* (plumbers), and repairmen are as hard to catch as a neuro-surgeon. Look for the ones that promise *pronto intervento* (prompt arrival). You will be charged usually for the call plus labour and parts.

MANAGING YOUR MONEY
Banks

Banks will gladly open an account in your name in euros or foreign currency. Where possible, choose an Italian bank that has a joint venture or partnership with your bank or a bank in your country. To receive money on your Italian account, send to your bank abroad: the name of the account owner, the street address of the branch of the bank where the account is located, and the account number plus the ABI and CAM numbers.

Some of the largest Italian banks, with offices nationwide, are San Paolo di Torino, Monte dei Paschi di Siena, Banca Commerciale Italiana, Banca Nazionale del Lavoro, Banca di Roma, and Banco di Napoli. Banca Popolare, Cassa di Risparmio, and Banca di Credito Cooperativo, roughly correspond to small savings and loans banks in other countries. Some foreign banks have offices, representatives, or branches in Italy. Here are some useful websites:

- **http://quotidiano.monrif.net/canali**
  For all economic news
- **http://wat.ch/termFinance/it**
  An extensive dictionary of words used in business and economics
- **http://www.bancaditalia.it**
  State agency supervising the world of banks
- **http://www.borsaitalia.it**
  Information on the Italian stock market
- **http://www.e-basta.it**
  A site critical of the new economy
- **http://www.re-mida.com**
  A finance search engine
- **http://www.uic**.it
  The *Ufficio Italiano Cambi* (the state office supervising exchange rates) offers current exchange rates.

Insurance Agencies

Get medical insurance before you leave for Italy. For your other needs, find out if your insurance company has connections, partners, or offices in Italy. It will make things much simpler.

Assicurazioni Generali is the largest Italian insurance company, with offices and agencies nationwide. Other companies operating nationwide are Alleanza, RAS, La Fondiaria, Cattolica Assicurazioni, INA Assitalia, Lloyd Adriatico, and Unipol Assicurazioni. Here are two useful websites:

- **http://guide.supereva.it/assicurazioni**
  A guide to the world of insurance
- **http://myinsurance.monrif.net**
  Offers and information from some of the top insurance companies around

Loan Advice

Ask your bank, both at home and in Italy. Be aware that most, if not all, banks will want collaterals and guarantees as well as a referent or counterpart in Italy. Remember the old aphorism: 'Banks give money to those who already have it.'

Tax and Legal Advice

Ask your embassy for a list of *Avvocati* (lawyers) and *Commercialisti* (commercial law graduates) familiar with *fiscalisti* or *tributaristi* (tax laws) and *internazionalisti* (international laws). For professional advice on tax, work, and non-profit matters, visit **http://www.consuline.it**. Some countries have treaties and agreements with Italy, concerning the taxation of foreigners working or living in Italy. Get information on fiscal and finance matters at the official site of the Istituto Nazionale Tributaristi:
http://www.vea.net or **http://www.tributaristi-int.it**

ENTERTAINMENT AND LEISURE
Bookshops & Libraries

- **http://www.aib.it**
  Associazione Italiana Biblioteche. Gives information and access to individual catalogues.
- **http://www.alice.it**
  Information from the Italian world of publishing
- **http://www.internetbookshop.it**
  The largest online bookshop, with some 250,000 titles

Cinemas & Theatres

- **http://www.trovacinema.it**
  Lists movie theatres city by city
- **http://www.cinemabaroni.com**
  Signor Baroni has the largest collection of movie posters, around 25,000 pieces.

Cultural and Social Organisations

Italy has an astounding number of cultural and social organisations. Look under *Associazioni artistiche* and *Culturali e ricreative* in the Yellow Pages. *Accademie* lists high-profile, often centuries-old academies in the arts and sciences and newer entities like the Accademia Italiana della Cucina (Viale Tunisia n. 48, Milan 20124), a non-profit body dedicated to the cultural promotion of Italian cuisine.

Health Clubs, Fitness Centres and Sports Facilities

Look under *Palestre, Fisiokinesiterapia,* and *Impanti sportivi* in the Yellow Pages. Check also for *Terme* (spas) near you. Italy has had a notable series of famous spas since Roman times.

Museums and Art Galleries

Visit **http://www.museionline.com** for a census of Italian museums by category and location. Find art galleries (private and commercial) in the Yellow Pages under *Gallerie d'Arte* for contemporary art or *Antiquari* for works of art from past centuries. If you buy important art or antiques, make sure you know if they are *notificati,* that is, in the list of goods of national interest. These cannot be bought or exported without the consent of the nearest Superintendent to the Fine Arts.

Nightspots

Look for *Discoteche, locali notturni,* nightclubs, and piano bars in the Yellow Pages. On the Internet:

- **http://www.salsa.gensoft.it**
  Latin American dance, with nightclubs, parties and classes nationwide
- **http://www.localionline.it**
  Has a list of night spots, with news and events
- **http://www.discotequeonline.it**
  Covers many nationwide discos, DJs, events, concerts and parades
- **http://www.discovillage.com**
  Addresses and information, region by region, province by province
- **http://www.romadinotte.com**
  Covers nightlife in Rome

Restaurants and Cafés

Look in the Yellow Pages under *Ristoranti* (also *Pizzerie, Trattorie, Birrerie e Pub*) and *Bar e Caffè*. Or visit **http://www.acena.it** for a listing of restaurants city by city.

Shopping

Italy is traditionally a shoppers' paradise. Each city has a main street with world-famous signature shops and usually a second area with lower prices and perpetual *svendite* (sales). There are hypermarkets and shopping centres outside many cities. Visit also the weekly outdoor markets and the *Grandi Magazzini* (Upim, Coin, Standa, etc.), some of which have websites, such as **http://www.rinascenteshopping.com**. For e-commerce, visit **http://www.commercenet.it, www.italia-shop.com**, or **http://www.spaziomercato.com**.

TRANSPORT & COMMUNICATIONS
Telephone Codes & Services

The phonebook lists *prefissi* for all Italian cities and foreign countries. Dial the Italian city code even when making local calls. Here are some telephone service numbers:

- **Directory assistance** (for phone number)   12
- **Directory assistance** (for name and address)   1412
- **International directory assistance**   176
- **Operator-assisted international calls**   170
- **Urgent calls**   197
- **Exact time**   161
- **Automatic wake-up call**   114

Internet Facilities and Cafés

Look under *Internet e servizi vari di informazione e intrattenimento* (Internet and various services of information and entertainment). Ask your Italian friends for new ones opening in your neighbourhood.

Post Offices

Found in every *Commune*. Listed in the phone book under *Poste Italiane*. The official nationwide website is
http://www.posteitaliane.it.

Transportation
Bus

Many companies operate bus services within and between cities. The urban ones are often familiarly called by the old name, tram. If you take the bus regularly, enquire about a weekly or monthly pass, or *abbonamento*. You can buy a ticket at the *Tabacchi*, marked by a 'T' sign, and sometimes at bars and newsstands.

Train

The Stazione Ferroviaria (train station) is usually called *Stazione* for short, but don't risk being sent to the *Stazione degli autobus* (bus station) instead. Buy your ticket at the counter and obliterate it at the small machine at the entrance to the platforms before you get on the train. For information and reservations, visit **http://www.fs-on-line.it**. Enquire about the new network of Eurostar fast trains which connects most of the main Italian cities.

Taxi

All cities have different numbers for radio taxi calls. Give a street address (if you are in the middle of a street, indicate a house or shop and stand in front of it) and you receive a confirmed answer with the number of the taxi picking you up. Italian taxi drivers do not have badges with photos, but they must have a number and meter. For long trips, such as to and from an airport, make sure you understand and agree on how the fee is calculated.

Mass Media

Refer to the following:

- **http://www.fnsi.it**
  The national press organisation, FNSI, lists press agencies, newspapers and radio stations.

- **http://www.mediaset.it**
  Mediaset, owned by the Berlusconi Group, operates TV channels Rete 4, Canale 5 and Italia 1.
- **http://www.rai.it**
  The Italian state broadcaster, RAI, operates television channels RaiUno, RaiDue and RaiTre, radio channels, and Rai Educational, producing cultural radio and television programmes.
- **http://www.windpress.com**
  Lists newspapers and magazines language institutes

Abroad

Before leaving for Italy, enquire about language courses at the nearest Istituto Italiano di Cultura (Italian Cultural Institute). There are over 90, in 61 countries, financed and supervised by the Italian Ministry of Foreign Affairs. They usually offer Italian language courses of high quality and at a moderate cost.

Alternatively, enquire at the foreign or Romance languages department of a university near you or at a private language school in your area.

In Italy

The two state Università per Stranieri (Universities for Foreigners) offer year-round classes at all levels in Italian language and culture, plus degrees in teaching foreigners Italian and certificates of knowledge and proficiency in Italian.

- **Università per Stranieri di Siena**
  Via Pantaneto,
  45–Siena 53100
  Tel: (0577) 240 111;
  Website: http://www.unistrasi.it

- **Università per Stranieri di Perugia** Piazza Fortebraccio
  4–Perugia 06100
  Tel: (0577) 732 236;
  Website: http://www.unistrapg.it

Alternatively, several universities offer language courses for foreigners, through their *Centro Linguistico* (language centre) and summer programmes. Or you may resort to a private language school.

RELIGION AND SOCIAL WORK
Religious Institutions

The Holy See is an independent state, with all juridical, diplomatic and social consequences deriving from it. Find all the references and addresses you need under *Città del Vaticano* in the Yellow Pages. As for the Catholic religion, the Italian territory, including city areas, is divided into *parrocchie* (parishes) run by a *parroco* (parish priest). *Parrocchie* form a *diocesi* (diocese) headed by a *Vescovo* (bishop) or *Arcivescovo* (archbishop). Look for *chiese* (churches) in the Yellow Pages. Other religions are classified as *chiese e centri di altri culti religiosi* and *religioni varie*.

VOLUNTEER ORGANISATIONS

Volunteer and charitable organisations operated and inspired by the Catholic religion, such as *Caritas*, are listed in the Yellow Pages under *Uffici ecclesiastici ed enti religiosi* (ecclesiastical offices and religious organisations). Other groups are classified as *Associazioni di volontariato e di solidarietà* (volunteer and solidarity organisations).

COUNTRY INFORMATION
Appliances and Utilities

Italy has a 220w electrical network. If you carry small appliances, such as electric razors, that work on the US or UK, you may need adaptors. These are generally not available at hotels; find them at *elettrodomestici* shops. You may consider bringing adaptors from home or buying battery-operated appliances.

Country Statistics

The best source is the *Annuario ISTAT*, published yearly by the state agency Istituto Centrale di Statistica (Central Institute of Statistics). Find this publication in or via libraries and bookshops or at Libreria dello Stato, bookshops selling publications of Italian state and state-related agencies. These are open only in major cities.

Embassies

Foreign embassies are located in Rome; Italian embassies usually in foreign capitals. Italy entertains diplomatic relations with practically every nation. Get a list of your country's diplomatic and official delegations (consulates, chambers of commerce, embassies, cultural institutions, university programmes) in Italy before departure.

General and Tourist Bureaus and Websites

The Ente Nazionale Italiano per il Turismo (Enit) is the national tourist organisation promoting tourism to Italy worldwide. The Compagnia Italiana Turismo (CIT) is the national Italian travel agency operating abroad.

In Italy, head for the Azienda Promozione Turistica (APT), which is the Tourist Promotion Agency, or the Proloco run by the local administration in all cities and towns. Tourist areas often have hotel promotion and tourist information stands or offices, operated by the different business categories. On the Internet:

- **http://www.600sec.com**
  Information on tourism in the northeastern area
- **http://www.medivia.it**
  Information on tourism in Campania
- **http://www.siena.turismo.toscana.it**
  The Siena APT website Government Internet Search Engines
- **http://www.comuni.it**
  A general site for local administration nationwide
- **http://www.governo.it**
  The Italian government website gives access to all ministers and ministries, such as the Ministero dell'Interno (Ministry of the Interior) at **http://www.cittadinitalia.it**. Regional governments also have their own websites.

IMMIGRATION, RESIDENCY AND NATIONALITY ISSUES

In 2003, the Italian Touring Club (TCI) counted 82 million new arrivals in Italy for a total of nights/presences of 344 million. The average number of nights spent in Italy by these 82 million is 4.19 nights per person.

The Ufficio Stranieri of the Questura in each province will provide information on residence policies and documents needed for living in Italy.

Necessities and Documents

Pre-entry vaccinations are usually not required, but this depends on your country. Enquire at the nearest Italian embassy or consulate. Bring your passport, medicine and prescriptions, health insurance valid in Italy, and an internationally-recognised ID issued by your state or local government. An international driver's licence issued in your country and a professional ID (such as a press or student ID) for professional contacts may be useful. If you are under treatment, carry enough medicine to cover your stay in Italy, or bring a clearly-written prescription. Bring your children's favourite thermometer. Remember this ironic adage: 'Travel light and with a heavy line of credit.'

WEIGHTS AND MEASURES

Italy uses the metric system. Here are some common conversion scales:

Distance

1 inch = 2.54 cm
1 foot = 0.305 m
1 yard = 0.914 m
1 mile = 1.609 km

Weight

1 lb = 453.60 g
1 oz = 28.35 g

Volume

1 imperial quart = 1.14 litres
1 U.S. quart = 0.95 l
1 imperial gallon = 4.55 l
1 U.S. gallon = 3.8 l

Temperature

Multiply degrees Celsius by 1.8 and add 32 to convert to degrees Fahrenheit. Subtract 32 from degrees Fahrenheit and divide by 1.8 to convert to degrees Celsius.

BUSINESS ORGANISATIONS

Each Italian province has an official chamber of commerce, grouping local firms engaged in commerce, industry, handicrafts (including small and cottage industry), and agriculture. Some foreign chambers of commerce have offices in Italy. Organisations for more specific categories include: *Confcommercio* for commerce, tourism, and services; *Confartigianato* for handicrafts; and *Confesercenti* mostly for shop owners and shopkeepers. Many business categories have websites, such as **http://www.plasticaitalia.com**, a guide to Italian industries engaged in plastics, with many links to individual firms.

EXPAT CLUBS

Ask your consulate or embassy for information. There are often formal or informal groups that provide social work opportunities including assisting other expats from your country and volunteer work in connection with Italian or international groups such as the Red Cross or Unicef. Groups of foreigners tend to form and gravitate towards embassies, consulates, churches, foreign chambers of commerce and culture institutes of their respective countries. Also, if you belong to clubs such as the Rotary, Lions or similar, find the local chapter of your club. You are usually welcomed and well-received instantly.

FURTHER READING

There are literally thousands of books about Italy. Here is a short selection dealing with some specific topics which you may find useful:

A Concise History of Italy. Peter Gunn. London: Thames and Hudson, 1971

A History of Contemporary Italy: Society and Politics 1943–1988. Paul Ginsborg. London: Palgrave Macmillan, 2003

A Traveller in Rome. H V Morton. Cambridge MA, USA: Da Capo Press, 2002

A Traveller in Italy. H V Morton. (with a new introduction by Barbara Grizzuti Harrison). Cambridge MA: Da Capo Press, 2002

A Traveller in Southern Italy. H V Morton. London: Methuen Publishing Ltd, 2002 (new edition)

Cadogan Guides: Italy. Dana Facaros and Michael Pauls. London: Globe Pequot Press, 1995

Chianti, The Land, the People and the Wine. Raymond Flower. London & New York: Christopher Helm Publishing Company, 1989 (revised edition)

Democracy, Italian Style. Joseph LaPalombara. New Haven CT, USA: Yale University Press, 1989 (reprint)

Getting It Right in Italy: A Manual for the 1990s. William Ward. London: Bloomsbury, 1991

Introduction to Italy. Vernon Bartlett. London: Chatto & Windus, 1967

History of the Italian People. Giuliano Procacci. London: Penguin Books Ltd, 2004

Italian Folklore, An Annotated Bibliography. Alessandro Falassi. New York: Garland Publishers, 1985

Italian Food. Elizabeth David. London: Penguin Books Ltd, 2005

Italian Labyrinth. John Haycroft. London: Penguin Books Ltd, 1987 (new edition)

Italy, A Modern History. Denis Mack Smith. Ann Arbor MI, USA: University of Michigan Press, 1969 (revised edition)

Live & Work in Italy. (Live and Work series). Victoria Pybus. Oxford, UK: Vacation Work Publications, 2005

Mafia and Clientelism: The Roads To Rome in Post-War Calabria. James Walston. Oxford, UK: Routledge, 1988

Passion and Defiance, Film in Italy from 1942 to the Present. Mira Liehm. Berkeley CA, USA: University of California Press, 1986 (reprint)

The Civilization of the Renaissance in Italy. Jacob Burckhardt. London: Penguin Classics, 1990

The Food of Italy. Waverley Root. New York: Vintage, 1992

The Italian Language Today. Anna-Laura & Guilio Lepschy. New York, USA: New Amsterdam Books, 1990 (2nd edition)

The Italians. Luigi Barzini. London: Penguin Books Ltd, 1991; New York, USA: Touchstone, 1996

The Italian Story: From the Etruscans to Modern Times. Geoffrey Trease. London: Macmillan, 1963; New York: Vanguard Press, 1964

The Stones of Florence and Venice Observed. (Penguin Travel Library series). Mary McCarthy. London: Penguin Books Ltd, 2000 (with a new edition released in 2006)

ABOUT THE AUTHORS

Raymond Flower got to know Italy during World War II. As a young infantry officer, he plodded martially up much of the peninsula until a mortar bomb, fired with no friendly intent, brought his foot-slogging days to an end.

For 35 years, he lived in a 12th-century Tuscan *castello*, producing his own Chianti wine. He also acquired an ancient mill in the Marche (see page 95), which was subsequently replaced by a hilltop estate between the sea and the Sibillini mountains. Formerly an international tennis player, car racer, and car constructor, he now divides his time between Italy and Southeast Asia.

A graduate of Magdalen College, Oxford, Raymond has written over 30 books, mainly historical, on a variety of subjects ranging from Egypt, Singapore and Western Australia to motor racing, winter sports and Lloyd's of London.

Raymond Flower is the author of *Chianti: the Land, the People and the Wine* and *Chianti: Storia e Cultura,* which received a Tuscan award. A history of the YMCA to mark its centenary in Asia was published in 2002 and he is currently working on a full-scale history of the Marche. His latest book *Playback: Writing An Autobiography* was published in 2003 to critical acclaim. *This Business of Writing* and *Napoleon to Nasser* have recently been published on the Internet.

Born into an old Tuscany family residing in Chianti and Siena since the Middle Ages, Alessandro Falassi was trained in Cultural Anthropology in Florence, Paris and later at the University of California Berkeley. As professor of Anthropology, he teaches in Italy and the United States.

Alessandro Falassi was the director of the University for Foreigners in Siena from 1985–1992. He taught anthropology on 'Semester at Sea' going around the world in 1979 and 1981. In 1988–1990, he directed the filming of Italian Festivals for the Italian Ministry of Culture.

Dr Falassi has published widely on social history, ritual and festivals, anthropology and folklore. His books are published in Italy, Spain, France, Germany, England and the United States.

In 1992, Alessandro Falassi was elected Prior of the Contrada Sovrana dell' Istrice in Siena where he lives with his wife and son when not travelling on his worldwide lecture tours.

Some of his published works are *Palio*, *Italian Folklore*, *Folklore By The Fireside*, *Time Out of Time* and *En la messa con Rossini*. In progress are *Hollywood's Italian Table* and *Italian Food in Los Angeles*.

INDEX

Titles in the CultureShock! series:

Argentina	France	Russia
Australia	Germany	San Francisco
Austria	Hawaii	Saudi Arabia
Bahrain	Hong Kong	Scotland
Beijing	Hungary	Shanghai
Belgium	India	Singapore
Bolivia	Ireland	South Africa
Borneo	Italy	Spain
Brazil	Jakarta	Sri Lanka
Britain	Japan	Sweden
Bulgaria	Korea	Switzerland
Cambodia	Laos	Syria
Canada	London	Taiwan
Chicago	Malaysia	Thailand
Chile	Mauritius	Tokyo
China	Morocco	Turkey
Costa Rica	Munich	United Arab
Cuba	Myanmar	Emirates
Czech Republic	Netherlands	USA
Denmark	New Zealand	Vancouver
Ecuador	Paris	Venezuela
Egypt	Philippines	
Finland	Portugal	

For more information about any of these titles, please contact any of our Marshall Cavendish offices around the world (listed on page ii) or visit our website at:

www.marshallcavendish.com/genref